Commendation for

JOURNEYS: Transitioning Churches To Relevance

"*JOURNEYS* by Duren and Wright is a book which will challenge, encourage, and even disturb readers. It is a brutally honest story of the struggle of two young pastors who yearn to see their churches impact culture for the cause of Christ in a way that is truly effective. Their struggles can be identified with most who have diligently sought to break out of traditional patterns and make a unique and powerful difference in reaching people for Christ. They desperately wanted to "be the church that God was calling us to be in our context and in our time." The struggles that they faced are honestly included. The lessons learned truly point to God's ongoing ministry to His servants.

It is a call to have a Kingdom philosophy of ministry as well as a missional approach to life. I commend this book to you. It is one that will help the next generation as they struggle in a less than easy environment in seeking to reach an ever increasing secular culture."

Dr. Frank Page, Senior Pastor, Taylors (S.C.) First Baptist Church Southern Baptist Convention President, 2006-2008

"*JOURNEYS: Transitioning Churches To Relevance* personifies the amazing persistence of God to graciously shape and effectively use us in His ongoing and always relevant work of restoring relationships with the highest order of His creation--people--of every tribe, tongue and nation. From a missionary point of view, it is a joy to learn of American pastors who are doing the same things that they would expect from foreign missionaries, namely to make whatever transitions are necessary in order to, in a culturally relevant way, faithfully communicate the fullness of God's love to the people of the host culture. Consider this book as a compelling, educational and transparent missionary journal of two pastors who have led their congregations to become both local and global missionaries to the current generations of unreached people living in the United States' Southeast and beyond. May their tribe increase!"

Jim Capaldo, Missionary to the Republic of Tuva, Siberia Russia Field Director, InterAct Ministries, Inc.

"Lots of people can tell you what to do. Some can do so through research, others through personal observation, and still others through their intuition. In *JOURNEYS: Transitioning Churches To Relevance*, Marty and Todd take us on a journey and tell us a story—and it is a worthwhile journey and a moving story. Instead of telling you what to do, Marty and Todd tell their journey from religious role-playing to personal transformation… and from personal transformation to fresh expressions of mission and ministry in their churches. I found myself engaged and challenged and believe you will as well."

Ed Stetzer, co-author of Comeback Churches *and* Compelled By Love

JOURNEYS

TRANSITIONING CHURCHES TO RELEVANCE

Todd Wright & Marty Duren

MISSIONAL PRESS

Published by Missional Press
149 Golden Plover Drive
Smyrna, DE 19977
www.missional-press.com

Printed in the United States of America

ISBN 13: 978-0-9798053-1-8
ISBN 10: 0-9798053-1-7

Cover art, concept and design by Sam Raynor.

Table of Contents

Acknowledgments

Todd would like to thank numerous people who have impacted his journey beyond measure: My wife, Lisa, who has provided a constant breath of fresh air since childhood, and who makes even difficult times wonderful to live through; my two awesome daughters, Hannah and Olivia, who constantly inspire me and deepen my commitment to reach the next generation; my parents, Alfred and Dean Wright, who, from childhood have taught me the Scriptures and to pursue the heart of God; the Midway family, who continue to follow their leader and walk by faith to be on mission with God in West Georgia and beyond; my fellow pastors, ministry directors, staff, deacons and executive officers at Midway who have lifted the load by leading and serving with joy, courage, and excellence; my co-author and friend, Marty, and friends, Wayne and Patty Payne, Don and JoAnn Williams, and Milford Collins who provide friendship, joy, and laughter virtually every week; and to Jesus, who has saved, gifted, and called me to make His mission mine.

Marty would like to thank his ever faithful and encouraging bride, Sonya, who "always knew you were going to write a book." I love you and could not have done it without you; Beth, Timothy and Abigail, three wonderful kids who were actually interested in what Dad was doing-you guys are awesome; the wonderful, adventurous body that is New Bethany (our best days are ahead!); Todd for being a true friend and for having patience during my writer's block; Blogger and Wordpress for making the blogosphere easy to enter so my writing skills could be honed; for each of the pastors who labored with me through the entire journey: Dan Brothers, Jr., Ron Cansler, Jr., Joey Jernigan and Brandan Lail and for those who were there part of the way, Danny Ashworth, Leonard Hinton and Jonas Wilson; my God and Father, triune Lord of the universe, maker of all that is, my friend and Savior.

We readily admit that this book would not exist without the valued knowledge and encouragement of David Phillips at Missional Press as well as the keen eye of Russ Rankin our editor who has made both of us look much smarter than we are. We are also grateful to the men who lent their influence to our project by virtue of endorsements.

Our awesome cover was designed by Sam Raynor. A gifted and passionate artist, Sam put our thoughts into a visual concept that is at once arresting and intriguing. The original watercolor that backs the tree/man silhouette is an abstract of the rings of a tree representing the different stages of the journey. For cover design or other art related interest she can be reached via email, sam@iamandsam.com.

Foreword by

Dr. Wes Griffin

Facts are always our friends. Facts may be pleasant. They may be painful. But, they are always our friends. Facts do not lie. They tell us the truth.

Todd Wright and Marty Duren faced the facts of our contemporary culture and the effectiveness of their churches. With their eyes wide open, they both charted a new course toward making a difference in their communities and the world.

This book will educate you, challenge you, and hopefully transform the way you and your church live. You will read about two pastors who searched their souls, passed out Godiva chocolates, meditated beside flowing rivers, challenged the status quo, and were willing to take risks in order to be found more faithful to Christ.

Today, God is looking for men and women who are willing to see a new vision, mobilize the body of Christ and overcome the obstacles to reach people with the life transforming power of the gospel.

Recently, I attended one of their churches. I thought, "this is not the same church that I attended three years ago. It is in the same building, but this is a different church." The service was full of energy, passion, and relevance. As I left the sanctuary, I was walking next to a visiting family, when I heard the son painfully say, "Dad, why is the church we normally attend so lame?"

Unchurched people are spiritually hungry and a contemporary movement of God is sweeping our nation. Wright and Duren are part of this movement. They are making the gospel relevant. This journey is not easy. It requires creativity and resolute determination. It involves risks and faith.

You and your church will either engage in this movement or you will be found sitting on the sidelines. I hope that you will join Wright and Duren on the journey. You will face the same challenges that they faced, yet you will also experience the same joy and you will be counted among those who are found faithful to God's call for this hour.

Dr. Wes Griffin

President, International Leadership Institute

The International Leadership Institute provides advanced Christian leadership training around the world. Alumni serve on the cutting edge of evangelism in more than fifty nations.

"The wind blows where it wishes, and you hear its sound, but you do not know where it comes from or where it goes. So it is with everyone who is born of the Spirit."
Jesus Christ to Nicodemus, a religious leader

"For what is our hope or joy or crown of boasting before our Lord Jesus at His coming? Is it not you? For you are our glory and joy."
The Apostle Paul to believers in Thessalonica

Introduction

Thanks for buying this book! We recognize that money is limited and for every book you buy you could have purchased another one. For that reason we are grateful that you chose our effort. We certainly hope that it will encourage you and bless your life and ministry.

The purpose for our writing is to tell our stories, our journeys if you will, of how we believe God called us to lead our respective churches to transition from traditional forms of ministry and missiology to more culturally connected forms of ministry and a better understanding of missional ecclesiology. This is not a "how-to-do-it" book; rather it is a "how-we-did-it" book written in narrative form. We write not to primarily provide a pattern, but to provide lessons for others who might desire a journey similar to ours, or who are already in the journey and are wondering if they will make it all the way through to the end. Each of the first six chapters covers the same subject matter as each of us alternately tells his story. By the way, all of our Scripture references are taken from the New King James Version of the Holy Bible.

Our journeys are similar and they are different, as are our lives and our churches. Todd Wright has been one of my closest friends for more than twenty years. I began working through the issues of transition before Todd did, but he, in my estimation, exhibited better leadership in implementing them. He read only about three books on the subject, while I read more than twenty volumes which, collectively, informed the totality of my thinking. Todd's church is in West Georgia, only twenty-five miles from Alabama, while mine is in suburban Atlanta, two miles from an "official" metro-Atlanta county. Midway Macedonia Baptist, the church Todd leads, experienced very rapid growth both before and after its transition; New Bethany Baptist, the church I pastor, has been slow to begin growing again after initially plateauing.

Both of these journeys are still in progress and neither of us claim any expertise in any area of transitioning a church. Since these *are* stories in progress, we will both forego some aspects that we might otherwise have told and omit specifics that we might otherwise have included. Our goal is not to offend but to inform.

We both feel as if our churches are the greatest churches in the world and each feels that the other is wrong, but we can both agree on this: We are better men for the churches we pastor and believe we are closer to God since these bodies decided to take these journeys with us. Passages of extreme candor should not be seen as negative toward our churches, but will hopefully be instructive to any pastor seeking to undertake such an endeavor as we have. **Please do**

not enter this journey lightly or not having counted the cost.

Though we each write of transitioning traditional churches, we both agree that traditional churches can be missional if that style of ministry is effective in reaching the surrounding culture. As David Putnam and Ed Stetzer write concerning the need to understand the culture, "It means discovering the principles that work in every context, selecting the tools most relevant for your context (which may come from methods and models), and then learning to apply them in a missionally effective manner."[1] Regarding how this relates to thinking like a missionary they continue, "They [missionaries] know that they must have a profound understanding of their host culture before planning a strategy to reach the unique people group that exists in that cultural context."[2] In each of our instances we felt as if the traditional style was ineffective, thus the transitions. The vision that moved both of us was to transition our churches to be biblically faithful bodies that connect culturally, influence locally and extend globally. It is this vision, only now put into words, which gave birth to the stories that follow.

[1] Ed Stetzer and David Putnam, *Breaking the Missional Code* (Nashville: Broadman and Holman), 2.
[2] Ibid, 2.

Authors' Note

All of these stories are told from memories that have been indelibly marked by the events. We have taken extreme care for accuracy, but, owing to the limitations of those memories, we admit that some events may not be in precise chronological order. For these and any other mistakes, we alone bear the responsibility.

BEGINNINGS

Chapter 1, part 1 (Todd)

Looking Back!

My spiritual journey began in a small town in West Georgia, and "church" has been a weekly part of my life as long as I can remember and before. Long before my time—from 1929 into the 1960s—my grandfather was the pastor of many of the churches in the West Georgia region. Sometimes he served as many as three churches at a time, because in those days most of them only had worship gatherings once a month, and it was often an all day affair. In addition to being the place for corporate worship, church was the community gathering place. For some, it was as much of a social event as it was an expression of faith.

During his era, my grandfather led churches during difficult days of change and transition. They had to face such issues and answer such questions as: "Should foot-washing remain a part of the church service?" "Would it be a disgrace to have indoor toilets attached to the 'sanctuary'?" "Why would a 'God-called' preacher need any education or use any notes when he preaches?" "Should a fellowship hall be connected to the sanctuary, and if so would that be considered eating in the church?"

Most of these things seem trivial to the modern day church, but they required major change for the churchgoers of the day in West Georgia. Some of these churches made the shift and transitioned toward a new way of doing the work of God. They were able to discern between cultural preferences and biblical patterns. Some experienced great revival and evangelism fervor in the 1940s and 50s, but some of them got smaller and smaller until they faded out of existence. Others experienced a church split and often a new dysfunctional church was born.

Today not much has changed except that perhaps the church is even less connected to the lives of mainstream citizens than sixty years ago. With the progression of professional wedding and funeral services, and Sunday as America's family day, many outside the church see almost no occasion to need the church or its message.

Good and Bad Experiences

Personally, I have very fond memories of my own church experience as a kid. Vacation Bible School, Easter egg hunts, children Christmas plays, Sunday School, baptism at Ward's Lake, handmade wooden pews, monthly business meetings, annual Sacred Harp singings and New Book singings, spring and fall revival. It seemed every season had its own excitement. Sunday was like a weekly reunion for me since most of my family and extended family attended the same church. My grandfather had once been the pastor. My other grandfather served as a deacon. My father was chairman of deacons. Both of my parents taught Sunday School. My grandmother played the piano, and almost everyone in the church sang in the choir. There was an "amen" corner made up of the leaders of the church. The "amen pews" sat sideways and, from where he sat, my father could keep a close eye on his four sons who were usually sitting in the back of the church.

I remember when the church where I grew up was vibrant and alive. People came to Christ regularly. There was a great spirit of worship and a vision of reaching people with the life-changing message of Jesus Christ. The altar was regularly filled with believers calling upon God to save a friend or put a family or a life back together again. Yet, within the last few years it has had as few as twenty-five people in worship attendance and seems to be perfectly content having the same few people attend their fellowship dinners and occasional Southern gospel singings.

As a teenager in the 1970s, I watched our church in the country struggle with the issue of "liberal" theology in our denomination. As a result, the church voted to sever their relationship with the denomination and it became an independent church where "legalism" soon began to take hold. We were taught by our pastor that to be in the denomination was to be "yoked together with unbelievers." The truly spiritual ladies should not wear anything but dresses, and the men should have a haircut with white-walls around the ears. If you heeded those two guidelines, and had a King James Bible, it seemed you were considered spiritual until proven otherwise.

I was attending college to become a mechanical engineer at the time, but a serious car accident awakened me to re-evaluate my spiritual life. I began to fast, pray and spend several hours a day in the Word. In the midst of that atmosphere, at the age of nineteen, the call of God moved upon my life to preach the gospel, and I began preaching in many of the same churches where my grandfather had once preached. People actually gave their lives to Christ after I preached, and the joy of being a tool to build God's Kingdom was firmly planted within me. After driving a forklift or working on machinery all week, I also taught the young adult Sunday School class, led the choir and congregational singing and served as the bus ministry director at our church. I was given instructions on how to handle the situation if a black person came to the door when I was inviting people to ride our bus to church. I was told to politely say, "I'm sorry. I'm at the wrong house." The Ku Klux Klan members occasionally stood on the street corner in our town to distribute literature for their cause; when I was sixteen, I had even gone to one of their meetings behind Whities' Tavern to hear about "saving" the white race. Since then, God had truly connected my heart with His regarding people, and my instructions for race relations in the bus ministry didn't seem right, especially for a church.

Launching as a Leader

Soon I was called to serve on a church staff in east Georgia. Very quickly I began to feel ostracized by my independent church comrades because of philosophical or cultural differences in doing ministry. That was the first time in ministry that I personally experienced the pain of political agendas and religious or cultural splintering, and it wouldn't be the last. Both at the denominational level and in the local church, it would be a constant challenge in ministry that I had never anticipated.

It was 1985, and I was twenty-one years old when I went to this new church and twenty-two when I left, but it seemed like ten years of experience to me. I served as bus ministry director and soul-winner for part of that time and minister of evangelism during another. I recruited and trained a team of about fifteen bus ministry leaders who performed with compassion and excellence every week. Annually, we were among the leaders in baptisms in our state convention, but soon found ourselves with less people in regular church attendance than we had baptized. It was a struggle for me to understand how we could be championed as successful with such results. I realized—in retrospect—that during one period of my tenure I was on a quota system. I was told that I had to have twenty people "down the aisle" for baptism within a one month period or I would not be paid. I met the mandate, but there was a hollow sense of personal accomplishment as a result instead of a sense of the movement of God. We sang choruses in that church which was the closest thing I knew of to a contemporary style of worship. I honestly never knew there was Christian music except Southern gospel, hymns or bluegrass.

The bus ministry that I was responsible for leading soon became a lightening rod for complaints and criticism. I had an awesome team of committed workers who visited in the neighborhoods every Saturday morning, and were on their buses on Sunday an hour and a half before and after church. Many children were ministered to, and many came to faith in Christ. For me and my wife, those days in ministry are some of our most treasured ever. I knew that the bus ministry would soon come to an end when one Sunday morning, a deacon asked one of my bus captains, "Why do ya'll keep bringing all of these black kids in here? They're tearing up the place!" Soon it was the subject of a deacon's meeting, and I was told to inform our regular riders that we would no longer bring them to church. I was told we didn't have "adequate facilities" for that type of ministry. I never understood their reasoning. Our church was a concrete block building!

A Bigger Arena of Leadership

In December of 1986, at the age of twenty-three, I began to serve on staff and later served as the senior pastor of a relatively large denominational church in south Metro Atlanta. There were more than two thousand members, but about six hundred regular worshippers. I served that church for almost ten years. I followed a very dominant leader who had served as their pastor for fourteen years. I got the idea that most of the people in the church would have followed him charging hell with a water pistol. I actually heard two or three leaders verbalize that statement. I, too, had great respect for him. He had a huge impact on my life and I considered it my privilege to serve on staff with such a leader. I had planned to serve alongside him in ministry for many years to come, but he announced his early retirement only a year and a half after my arrival. When he retired from the pastorate, he recommended me to be the next pastor, which I accepted. It was an extremely difficult and challenging time in my life, but it was the pressure-cooker that would increase my capacity to deal with difficulty and personal pain.

I lived in the shadow of my predecessor, who was a spiritual giant to many of the people I served. Others seemed to despise him and were glad he was gone. The church was in decline. There were financial problems. The staff had to be downsized. Our Christian school was growing, but had financial problems and needed to be restructured. I did not have the same leadership style and personality as my predecessor. It was the first time in my life I had served in the "senior leadership spot." At the age of twenty-four, I was the youngest and least experienced on staff. I actually knew little about transitioning or any other component of leadership; but I was the leader and had to make numerous difficult and unpopular decisions.

Worship was led with a piano, organ and orchestra, backed by the robed choir. Worship was followed by hopefully good preaching and an invitation. We were back for a different sermon on Sunday night, except the crowd was about 75 percent smaller, and everyone who came on Sunday night had also been present on Sunday morning. I led an additional Bible study on Wednesdays. Each day, I was in the office Monday through Friday from eight in the morning until five o'clock in the evening. I sometimes visited church prospects two other nights a week and on Saturdays.

The pace of life, the pressures of leadership, constant attempts to match up to people's expectations, and the lack of identifiable success often led me to feelings of frustration, failure, and depression. While I never allowed myself to consider taking my own life, there was many times I told God I didn't want to live anymore. On one occasion I told my chairman of deacons that I desperately needed a month off, but he quickly reminded me that I did not have that much vacation time. On another occasion, I actually had my resignation written, intending to quit ministry altogether. I rationalized that if this was what ministry was all about, I wanted no part of it.

Becoming Kingdom Focused

One day during that time period, Dr. Billy Britt, a friend and professor of mine, called and encouraged me to attend a leadership seminar where Dr. John Maxwell would be teaching basic leadership principles. Another seminar was the last thing on my mind, but as a "last hope," I went anyway. I sat and wept as I wrote things that became life transforming for me. God used that phone call and event to keep me from quitting ministry altogether. In addition to learning great principles of leadership, I was also exposed to other pastors and church leaders from other denominations. Many of them were facing some of the same challenges I was facing. Some of them led churches with models of ministry that were traditional in nature and others were contemporary in nature.

Call me sheltered if you want, but that was the first time I understood that someone could do ministry differently or be something other than from my own denominational heritage and still be right with God. Even though I was becoming more of a Kingdom-focused leader, I still had my problems with many things identified with a different way of doing church. I regularly preached so as to protect the integrity of my way of doing church; but inside I would never see the "the church" or "the body of Christ" in the same way as before. I came back from that seminar with the principles and strategy to lead our church to the next phase of our journey.

Among other endeavors, I had led the church to be more personally involved in seeing, giving, and going to building God's Kingdom. I had gone to Liberia in West Africa in 1987 and really began to see that God's church was so much bigger than I had ever dreamed. That trip was the beginning of a passion and vision inside of me to reach the nations with the gospel. I continue to live with that passion and vision every day, and West Africa continues to be a special place in my heart. On one occasion my family actually applied with our denomination to be missionaries, but it wasn't in the plan of

God. I did, however, lead our church to be personally involved in mission work and evangelism there and in several other places throughout the world.

I had several more years of ministry through that church, and together we saw some good things take place. However, I'll always be convinced that the greatest changes and progress took place inside of me. I learned about the importance of leading through a compelling vision, and my capacity for dealing with difficult problems and sometimes difficult people had increased greatly.

Throughout my tenure there, I invited some of the best preachers and leaders to speak at our church. We grew by a couple of hundred people in average attendance. We were one of the leaders in baptisms in our state convention. When I left, the church was in good shape financially and had fifty additional acres and several thousand square feet of additional space in which to do ministry. However, there was an obvious power struggle among a few deacons in the church, which openly manifested soon after I resigned, and a mass exodus occurred during the following year. For me personally, I felt numb inside, and any feeling of true success faded in light of the destructive power struggle that followed. It had been a difficult ten years with few opportunities to be refreshed. Looking back, as my ministry at that church came to a close, I honestly think I needed a mental hospital or a long vacation, neither of which I received.

A New Opportunity

In June of 1996 I became the pastor of a much smaller church in west Georgia. It's the church I continue to lead. At the time of this writing, Midway has celebrated its 160th anniversary. It was started by a true church planter, Rev. Leroy McWhorter, July 15, 1847. His direct descendants are still active members. It was started as "The Baptist Church of Christ at Macedonia" and later became Macedonia Baptist Church, then Midway Macedonia Baptist Church. Even though there have been no more official name changes, we are now commonly just called Midway-A Five Star Focused Church.

When I arrived, the church had about 185 people in Sunday School and 220 people in worship. After serving a church with several hundred people, and being responsible for almost 100 employees in the church and school, this new place of service seemed very appetizing to my wounded mental and emotional state of mind.

I was the only full-time staff member. I had no set office hours. There was no computer, no current constitution and bylaws, no big budget to meet, no one to supervise, and—until just before my arrival—no active deacon ministry. However, one thing they did have was a vision and passion to grow and reach people. My predecessor at Midway, Pastor Jesse Leonard, had faithfully served there for ten years before retiring at the age of seventy. He was a visionary leader who had led the church from sixty-eight in attendance to more than 200. He had challenged them to find a younger pastor and to reach the next generation of young families. He informed them that the growth of Atlanta would reach them over the following years, and that they needed to be prepared to be as effective as possible. Most of the people who served under his leadership have been some of my greatest encouragers and supporters through each major transition of change. His influence and positive vision continue to be a part of the fabric that makes Midway who she is.

Before accepting the pastorate at Midway, there were several questions I asked the search committee. These questions had to be answered to my satisfaction or I would not accept the position. Among them were these questions:

1. What is your understanding of the role the pastor?
2. What's required of the pastor that nobody else can do?
3. How is the church governed?
4. What is your understanding of the role of deacon?
5. Is every race of people welcome as a part of the church?
6. Are you willing to change the name of the church? (I wanted to test their flexibility.)
7. Is there any one family that's known to run the church? If so who are they?
8. What's your vision of what the church should be and do?
9. What's the history of the church?
10. Have there been any splits? If so, when and why?

It was an awesome experience as I watched these leaders address my questions with openness and integrity. They were reasonable, flexible, and obviously wanted their lives to count for the Kingdom of God. They had a spirit about them that connected with me. They were the kind of people I wanted to grow old with as we served God together. On the way home from my first meeting, my wife and I knew these were the people with whom we wanted to work to serve in God's Kingdom. It hasn't always been easy for them, or me, but the journey together has been pretty awesome. Most members of the search committee, who are still alive, continue to be a part of the journey.

For some reason God has placed me in two churches where heritage and history run deep and tradition dies slowly. The last year before I left my previous pastorate, we celebrated the church's 150th anniversary. In each case, I am honored to have been a part of an institution that has been an oasis of faith for so many years. However, as I have served both churches, hidden somewhere down inside me there has been a deep sense of duty to keep all of the components of the traditional model of church planted firmly in place. These components included Southern gospel music or hymns, top-of-the-line suits with ties, and a worship culture that would be described more as reverent entertainment rather than participative celebrative worship. I still believe all of those things are great, as long as they fit the culture of the people that a church is attempting to reach. My problem was in the fact that I viewed my way of worship as *the* biblical way, and every other culture or style as unbiblical.

During my first pastorate I remember being championed by elder statesmen to keep things the way they

28

had always been, and for many years I did. I have passionately preached against almost everything and everyone (by name) identified with changing the church from its traditional model to a more culturally connected model. I received many amens and words of encouragement. I saw it almost as "contending for the faith once delivered to the saints." Now don't get me wrong. We saw people come to Christ and we experienced some growth, but even when I was in my twenties as a senior pastor we had great difficulty getting young adults integrated into the life of the church for any length of time. It was hard for me to understand that I was often preaching against culture, rather than using culture to connect people to God. I had made several trips to other countries, and in each case was taught to be culturally sensitive, and use culture to introduce people to Jesus Christ. However, when in North America I was ignoring the value of culture and preaching against it.

At Midway I had a unique opportunity to start over at the age of thirty-one, and from day one, on "Welcome the New Pastor Sunday," the church was full. Several came to Christ that first month, which seemed to be a good affirmation of God's hand upon us. Within three months of our initial journey together, we started a second Sunday morning worship service. We had a prayer emphasis in which we drove down every street within a five-mile radius of our church, and prayed for those who lived in every home. A year later we visited and left literature at every home within a five-mile radius. We took mission trips to Brazil and West Africa.

The people at Midway were very much like those who labored with Nehemiah: "They had a mind to work" (Neh. 4:6). All of the prayer and labor paid off. We continued to grow at double-digit rates every year. We built new facilities. We put an Acts 1:8 strategy in place, through which a deacon took responsibility for our mission impact in each part of the world. We were effectively doing ministry in our own community and around the world. We planted a church in our county a few miles away. We joined with some other churches to plant a church in Las Vegas. We also planted a church in the country of Belgium, where less than half of one percent of the population are evangelical believers. We were listed consistently as one of the fastest growing Sunday Schools in our state convention. However, hidden beneath the surface of our success was the fact that a large majority of our growth was from people who were already churched and were simply looking for a new one. Soon, I would be confronted with an even bigger piece of life-changing information that lurked all around me, and as a result I would be moved into a new spiritual crisis. Once again I would never be able to view the church the same as before, and I would have to make some difficult decisions as a result.

Chapter 1, part 2 (Marty)

"[The] research indicates that most people who do not go to church do not attend for clear and specific reasons.

*Their problem is not with Christian theology; **it is with how
we do church.** [Emphasis in original]*[1]

James Emery White

First Things

Church history, for me, began when I was three years
old. On a Thursday night, men from a growing local church in
Lake City, Georgia, came to our apartment and shared the
gospel with my mother while my dad was at work at the Ford
Motor Company assembly plant. At my age, and being more
concerned with missing *The Flying Nun*, I was unaware that
she was faced with the reality of her sin and had accepted
Christ. Shortly thereafter, my dad also professed Christ and
though he would not actually come to faith in Christ for
another three decades, we quickly began regular church
attendance at that church at that time.

As a member of the Duren family, I found myself
participating in everything that the church had to offer. There
is a photo of me in the children's choir, I was in the nursery
for Tuesday morning visitation, and we were at every service
of every revival meeting, Sunday School and Training Union.

From 1966 until 1976 we attended that same church,
until a disagreement over a new pastor's theology took us to a
neighboring town and Mt. Zion Church in Jonesboro, Georgia.
It was at Mt. Zion that I came to know Jesus Christ and

---

[1]- James Emery White, *Rethinking the Church* (Grand Rapids: Baker
Books, 1997), 19.

responded to God's call on my life to the pastoral ministry.

Being in these two churches through all my formative emotional and spiritual years, I experienced what would commonly be termed *traditional* styles, organizational structures, music, dress, preaching and basic ecclesiology. *Change* was not a word on anyone's mind and the only thing contemporary was an Easter "cantata" that was done on stage in costume rather than in the choir loft.

There was really no reason to question anything as we were doing church the way we knew was right. There was nothing to cause anyone to question the philosophy of ministry under which church life took place, as it was identical to 98 percent of small town churches across the nation. The choir more than likely wore robes, the piano and organ were always in full swing (if there was enough money to pay musicians), revival would include lunch meetings, there was preaching on Sunday morning, night and Wednesday night, hair was short and services were long.

I had been taught that loving God meant to be separate from worldliness (which is right), to be separated from the world (which is right, rightly understood) and the best way to do that was to avoid contact with worldly people (which is totally wrong). In a distinct memory of a Christian camp while I was in high school, the counselor challenged me to go home and dump all of my unsaved friends. Though I dealt with guilt over it, I did not dump them and, though they did not affect me adversely, neither did I affect them very much for the Lord.

So steeped was I in the traditions of the church that, from my high school years, I listened to no secular music; indeed I believed it possible (even probable) for demonic presences to be in anything other than Southern gospel quartet music. Keith Green's *Dear John Letter to the Devil* was quite a point of consternation for me, though eventually the biblical lyrics of Dallas Holm and Petra began to open my mind to a new possibility that other music styles might actually be glorifying to God. As in my early preaching years, I preached against any sin the Bible condemned and a few that God had forgotten.

And so it was, that when I was called as a pastor in 1989, I carried much of this philosophy with me. My first full-time ministry opportunity was a little "family owned and operated" church out in the country about 45 minutes south of Atlanta. We sang hymns with great effort and I decked out in the best clothes that I could afford. A great transition was accomplished when we removed the "Doxology" from weekly use in the service. I fully believed that verse-by-verse exposition through entire books of the Bible was the only God-approved way to preach and so in my short tenure I made it through Philippians, Jonah, John and Revelation (on Wednesdays).

My greatest break with tradition was that I did not "dress up" on Wednesday nights since I was also preaching a youth service after the adult Bible study time. I was schooled in a theology of pastoral authority that I now recognize bordered on dictatorship and caused a few headaches that I need not have suffered. I knew nothing about delegation or team building and my duties entailed answering the phone, filling the baptistery, typing and printing the weekly bulletin as well as visiting, preaching and walking on water. It was a typical country church pastorate.

After more than a year and driven by a burden to reach more of our community, I presented a growth plan to the church with an emphasis on having an "open door policy" to all races. It was met with all the excitement of a non-anaesthetized hemorrhoid surgery. That attempt was also the beginning of the end of my two-year tenure as pastor.

Following those rough two years at that first church, we planted a new church in the same town. We met at the local skating rink, though that did not stop me from wearing a suit each week while preaching with an occasional wrestling ring pushed off to the right, evidence of the previous night's mayhem. Ladies in Sunday dresses and kids with leather shoes filled in our fifty or so seats each week to hear me preach my hardest sermons.

New Place, Same Style

Later, another opportunity took me to a mobile home park mission church to serve among some pretty poor people. Rent in the ramshackle dwellings was about one hundred dollars a week. It was the last stop before the street, although some people actually made it their family home for a long, long time. That was not true of the majority who were living a transient lifestyle owing to too much drink or drugs or too little work ethic.

I think back as to how goofy I must have looked each week wearing my suit into this building where the music was provided through an electronic music machine called a "Hymn Player." Programmed to match the songs in the Baptist Hymnal, one could merely punch in the appropriate number and out, through the dime store speaker set, came a monstrous rendition of poor Fanny J. Crosby's best effort. It sounded like some demented Phantom of the Opera had taken over the organ. Nevertheless, I stood and led as best as I could.

The pews in the building had been donated and unfortunately the previous owners had a much wider building than ours. Of course, the only rational thing to do to make these slatted benches fit was to divide them with a chainsaw, or that's how it appeared. So, even though they came to fit the room, each one had one rough-cut end: one against the wall and the next into the room. The ends were not the only things rough cut—so were the seats. One Sunday, while wearing a woven style blazer, I arose to make announcements only to find that a 6-inch slice of pew had lodged itself in the weave, broken loose and gone to the pulpit area with me! From then on, I leaned forward when I sat down. In God's grace, these were eventually replaced with better pews donated by my home church.

We had one Louisianan family that attended the mission—a mom and her two kids. The boy, Travis, could not speak any English, but his Cajun was impressive. The girl, who was three or four, liked to do basic training while I was preaching. She would start at the back and go alternately over and under the pews until reaching the front. On one occasion Travis picked up a hymnal and, in the middle of my message, walked up beside me, opened it and began to mimic me preaching. Knowing that the only reason he did it was because he respected me, I just smiled and kept going.

I tell these stories because through the first months, I was still wearing suits and nice shoes, flashy ties and preaching like the pastor search committee from First Church of Somewhere, USA, was sitting in the back. Incongruent would not be an inappropriate word to describe the situation.

Finally, at a point that I do not even remember, I thought, "Why am I wearing a suit and tie to preach at a place where most of the people are struggling to afford food and clothes?" So, just like that, I quit. I do not remember if I wore jeans or just lost the jacket and tie, but it was the first time that I can recall in ministry where I made a conscious decision to stop something that might inadvertently be a hindrance for someone to come to Christ. I knew that the gospel by its nature was a stumbling block, but I had not realized how much I—myself—might be a stumbling block if I paid no attention to the culture of those around me. It would be many, many years before that thinking grabbed me and refused to let go.

On a Pastoral Staff

In the spring of 1992 I began serving on staff at a church northeast of Atlanta in fast-growing Gwinnett County. A true megachurch, God had grown this huge body in what was then the middle of nowhere. It was a truism that you only went past it if you meant to go there, because no one would ever go that direction by accident. (My mission church assignment was actually part of my job description of this larger church.)

Though it was considered by many to be a contemporary church, it had some very traditional elements. A strong choral ministry of graded choirs and praise teams, "Sunday dress," the pulpit as the center of the building and the sermon as the center of the service. Though unconventional in some of its functional structure, it was very conventional in its strategy: get as many people on campus as we could and when we had too many, either build another building or rent some school space down the road. To use Frost and Hirsch's terminology, it was an "attractional-evangelistic" church rather than a "missional-incarnational" church. In fact, most of the churches I had ever attended were from the "attractional-evangelistic" philosophy as were the church growth books I had studied and the conferences I had attended, thus it formed the core of my own ministry philosophy. (For full explanations of these terms, I recommend *The Shaping of Things to Come*, by Michael Frost and Alan Hirsch.)

New Pastorate

In April of 1998, God saw fit for me to be called to New Bethany Baptist Church in Buford, Georgia, a growing bedroom community in North Atlanta. Located in Hall County, immediately adjacent to Gwinnett County, the fastest growing county in the entire US for much of the decade of the 1990s, we were poised for growth if for no other reason than the wave of new people moving out of Gwinnett into Hall. As my other ministry positions, this church was traditional in most of its elements of worship, even though most of our members considered it "blended" since a few songs like "Majesty" were incorporated along with the hymns.

Traditional, in reality, was the best descriptor: robed choir, Sunday School, evening worship, Wednesday prayer meeting, RAs and GAs, piano and organ. Dress was almost without fail the "Southern Baptist Sunday Best" variety, even though we were mere minutes from a large lake resort and that culturally laid-back way of thinking. My alliterated "three points and a poem" style of preaching was well received and almost immediately *church members* began to be saved.

As a matter of fact, early in my ministry at New Bethany, there was a stretch of time when we had some kind of decision for Christ—a profession of faith, transfer of membership or baptism—at least once a week for several months, continuing the early pattern of many already churched people coming to Christ. It was the best of times and the honeymoon was sweet. Workers were plentiful, attendance was growing, everyone seemed happy, we baptized more than forty the first year and more than thirty the second year.

But after a while, something began to eat at me. Badly. People were still being saved and baptized and we had grown from about 185 in Sunday School on my first Sunday to averaging better than three hundred for the period of our *40 Days of Purpose* emphasis. We had baptized in the neighborhood of 125 in my first four years, but baptisms were declining slowly each year. Annual attendance patterns could be laid on top of each other, as virtually the same cycle repeated from fall to winter to spring to summer.

It was this realization that brought me to a point of crisis that I never expected and from which I never returned.

CRISIS

Chapter 2, part 1 (Todd)

Living Every Pastor's Dream

It was the spring of 2003, and Midway had become the church I had always dreamed of leading. We had grown by at least 10 percent in Sunday School ever since I had arrived in 1996. One year we had grown by 32 percent and our average annual Sunday School growth was 19.5 percent. Our offerings had grown at an even higher rate. We had lots of new people and plenty of money with which to do ministry. We built all new facilities that would be paid for by the end of 2005, and now we were having two Sunday morning worship services and two Sunday School hours to accommodate the growth. We were in the early stages of designing our next phase of facility expansion, which would be a youth, children and preschool facility at an estimated cost of $9 million. We had a large mission budget on top of giving through our denomination's missions programs. We literally had hundreds of our people personally involved in ministry and missions work at home and abroad. We helped establish an ongoing baseball ministry in Brazil. We led leadership training and Vacation Bible Schools in West Africa. We helped plant a church in Las Vegas and in Belgium. We also planted a new church in our own community. Besides all of that, there was no contention in the church. The deacons were more concerned with ministry than playing church politics, and the people definitely had a mind to work. What more could a pastor want? I felt I was living out every pastor's dream. Our journey together had been truly therapeutic.

A Philosophical Struggle

When we prepared to start the new church in west Georgia, we took a fairly unselfish approach. We simply asked for volunteers who felt called to be on mission with God to start a new church. The only requirements were that they had to tithe and serve. There were some awesome people who felt called to go, including two deacons. It was another exciting step as we planned for a new church. It was something that so few people and churches are ever a part. We partnered with a church planter who felt called to plant a church in the area and brought him on staff for approximately a year, so he could build his core team.

He had grown up in the west Georgia area, and then graduated from Georgia Tech and Dallas Theological Seminary. I knew he understood the culture and had the training for such a venture. He had gone through the appointment process and had been approved by our denomination. He obviously had the calling and passion for the task.

However, I recall struggling through some of my initial conversations with him about the philosophy and style of this new church. He felt called to plant a contemporary kind of church with a strategy to "turn irreligious people into fully devoted followers of Christ." This would include casual dress, drama, video clips, no Sunday night service, music other than Southern gospel or hymns, and a modern translation of the Bible. Through the years, I had preached against all of those things, and felt like they were the ruin of the "true Church." Now Midway was going to help promote and pay for the establishment of such a church. I didn't make it public, but I really struggled with it. "It might draw a crowd, bless God, but it just isn't Biblical!" I argued. Somehow I was confident that Southern gospel music, suits with ties and a Sunday night service was almost commands from holy writ.

Even though I disagreed with his philosophy and style of ministry, we continued in our partnership. I am glad we did. At the time of this writing, Peachtree Community Church has just entered their new facilities. Their pastor, David Reid, has done an awesome job as a leader; may he forgive me for my possible ignorance or arrogance at the time. I am honored to have been a small part of their journey.

Life-Changing Information

As a result of Midway being a church committed to help start other churches, I was invited by our denomination to speak at a Church Planting Conference in south Georgia. We had launched one new church in our community, and I was an expert already.

After I spoke, I hung around for the other sessions. A denominational employee gave some statistics showing the few percentages of south Georgia residents who attend church on a given Sunday. I was saddened to see that only ten to seventeen percent of the population of most counties in south Georgia attended a church. These statistics included the churches and places of worship for every religious group such as Mormon, Jehovah Witness or Islam.

I was confident that the statistics in Carroll County, where I served as pastor, were much higher. It seemed like there was enough people standing in the buffet line on Sunday afternoon at Ryan's Steakhouse to fill up several churches.

At the close of the conference, I asked for the statistics for Carroll County. I was floored to find that only 14.4 percent of Carroll County's residents attended a church each weekend. While I never really knew the facts, and never sought to find out, I had always assumed that forty to sixty percent were closely connected to a church. Now it suddenly dawned on me that I led a church in what is often referred to as the Bible Belt; but for the majority of people, the church was not even showing up on their radar screen. Most of the growth Midway had experienced consistently dipped into that same 14.4 percent, as people who already knew Christ came to join our exciting church. We snuggled all cozily and warmly each Sunday in a culture that was totally secluded from the people we were sent to reach. Almost eighty-six percent of our county's population drove past the different churches in the community every day, but saw no reason to drive into the parking lot on the weekends. Because of our fast and continue growth, Midway was often championed as a huge success story, but at that moment I realized how ineffective we had actually been.

As I drove home from that conference, I tried to think of why the church that was so important to me was not connecting to those who needed it most. On at least four different occasions, we had knocked on every door within a five-mile radius of the church. We had also handed out fifty thousand invitation "Care Cards" face to face over a twelve month period. We had a weekly visitation program and delivered homemade pies and cookies to those who had visited the church the previous weekend. We constantly worked to keep our Sunday School organized and growing. I knew of some other churches in the area that appeared to be trying just as hard as we were, but for some reason, it seemed the church as a whole had no real attraction for those without Christ.

Actually thirty-three percent of our county's residents claimed membership in a church, but obviously more than half of them no longer attended. That meant there were two major problems. Many people were de-churched and even more were unchurched. Many people I had invited to Midway could tell of a time when they used to go to church. They used to sing in the choir or teach Sunday School. When asked why they no longer attend, they usually attributed it to a particular "business meeting," a moral problem, hypocrisy, boredom, or a leadership problem.

By the time I arrived home from the conference, I knew I had faced another defining moment in ministry perspective, but I still didn't realize what changes would be required of me in the days ahead. I was so moved by this new information that I passionately shared it with my church the following Sunday. I also sent a letter containing the information to every evangelical church in the county. I knew I had to do something with this information, but in all honesty I didn't know what.

At one point Midway sponsored a steak dinner for pastors who would come and discuss partnering together for an area-wide event to connect people to Jesus at one of our high schools. I offered a free set of Dr. John Maxwell's leadership books to everyone who would attend the dinner. The big event would host several contemporary Christian bands including a Christian rapper, extreme games, food, fun, and a clear presentation of the gospel. About fifteen of our 123 churches in the county jumped in to help, and the event was a success, but most pastors ignored the opportunity. Some actually preached against the event or refused to participate, because it wasn't "their kind of music." Others boycotted the event because I invited churches from all denominations to participate. One "Christian" school called a special meeting with parents to forbid their children to attend. Another church actually brought a group to the event with picket signs to protest against the event. However, for those who participated, bridges were built across racial, religious and cultural barriers in the community.

Honest Evaluation

Over the next several months I found myself questioning virtually everything I had ever been taught or believed about the church. I knew the church could be so much more than what we were experiencing. When Jesus said, "I will build my church and the gates of hell will not prevail against it" I was convinced He meant more than a place where we heard a few songs and a sermon.

I had always believed the church was the hope of the world, and I still do believe that. However, if the church was suppose to be a "hospital for sinners instead of a hotel for saints," as Evangelist Vance Havner use to say, most of the churches I knew of, including mine, were a miserable failure. Most churches have few in attendance, and it's usually the same people week after week. Most attendees seem to have a fairly small worldview. They quickly complain about everything they don't like in the church service, as if they paid their money for a big weekend show that ended up being a disappointment. By the way, did I mention that most of those in attendance in the average church are above the age of fifty? Usually, those under the age of fifty who do attend are those who were "raised in the church" as children—that group is quickly dwindling, as well.

As I thought about all of these things, it was beginning to sink into my thick pharisaical skull that the average church had evolved into little more than an exclusive club. Some were wealthy clubs and some were middle-class or poor clubs. Some were white clubs and others were black, Latino or Asian, but exclusive clubs they were. Each had a weekly demonstration of cultural talent, followed by a sermon preached to people who had already professed Christ.

Seldom does anyone bring an unbeliever to church and most churchgoers seem to feel totally incapable of, or uninterested in developing friendships with unbelievers throughout the week. Too often, the major identifier of "the Spirit of God moving" takes place when a person is moved to tears when their favorite song is sung, much like when Elvis sang "How Great Thou Art," or possibly when the preacher tells a sad story. Everyone who attended can then go home and say, "We sure did have a good service today." I had to ask myself, "Is that why Jesus died--so we could have good church services?"

If God is so great and hell is real, how can churchgoers be content making little or no impact in the lives of those who need Jesus, just as long as their kind of music is played or sung, and the preacher wears a suit and tie while preaching from behind a big pulpit? Literally thousands of churches throughout America have church services fifty-two weeks out of the year and do not see even one single person come to know Christ. But many times they'll be pleased that they "had a good church service." Other churches may baptize hundreds of people, yet remain virtually the same size year after year. In our case we were growing by great numbers but were reaching very few unchurched people. After a year with no real impact, most will not even stop to evaluate what, why and how they are doing. They continue to do the same thing year after year expecting a different result. They simply hope that some day *it* will just happen, and something will change.

I was now preaching to myself and I knew I needed to repent, which I did. It was both a humbling and sometimes confusing time, but I knew God had awakened me to the lost condition of mankind again. I had allowed many of the traditions of my personal culture to become as important to me as the very commands of Scripture. In many cases it was difficult for me to know the difference. Besides, many of my favorite preachers and heroes of the faith had affirmed my philosophy of ministry for many years. I knew if I changed, some of them would accuse me of compromising the faith, going "liberal," or going through a midlife crisis. I had heard all of these things before. Sometimes they had come from my own lips regarding others. In many ways I felt like Saul the Pharisee before he became the Apostle Paul. In my zeal to honor God and to maintain a pure faith, I was very zealous for a lot of things that were not biblical, but cultural. Many of those things had become the very walls that were keeping the unchurched out of the church. Because of my own emotional weaknesses and insecurities, I had often been a part of the problem of the church instead of leading the church to engage humanity with the gospel. I had helped develop an organization where Christians could separate themselves and feel safe from the world every week, rather than engage the world with the love and claims of Christ.

A Double Whammy

About a year later, I was confronted by some more startling facts of research. I was reading a great book by Reggie McNeal entitled *The Present Future-Six Tough Questions for the Church*. In it, he published the findings reported by Dr. Thom Rainer that got my attention.

> "Thom Rainer of the Billy Graham School of Evangelism at Southern Baptist Seminary reports some disturbing responses to the two frequently asked Evangelism Explosion questions ("do you know for certain that if you died today you would go to heaven?" and "If you were to die today, what would you say to God if He asked you why He should let you into His heaven?"). The interview included about 1,300 persons of each of four generational groups that Rainer identified and investigated (5,200 in all). Analyzing the responses for evidence that the respondents were born again (the evangelical definition of one's being a Christian) yielded the following results: builders (born before 1946)—65 percent; boomers (born between 1946 and 1964)—35 percent; busters (born between 1965 and 1976)—15 percent; bridgers (born between 1976 and 1994)—4 percent. Those interviewed in the bridger category were at least seventeen years old."[1]

[1]- Reggie McNeal, *The Present Future-Six Tough Questions for the Church* (Jossey-Bass: San Francisco), 4.

As I stared wide-eyed at this information, I fully realized that while Rainer's survey did not represent a scientific statistical sampling, it certainly appeared that a very negative trend was developing for the North American church. I remembered that for many years research has shown that a large majority of people, who come to know Christ, do so before the age of twenty-five. The trend pointed to the reality that unless something changes, we are only a few years away from being a post-Christian nation. Some would argue that we have already arrived to that condition.

Exposing Keys Players to the Facts

As a result, I began to ask my staff and some of our church leaders some important questions:

- Why have we grown so much, but baptized so few?
- Why has most of our growth been from those age forty and up who are white, middle-class and/or who have a church background?
- Why do we seldom reach anyone who is truly unchurched and them stay for any length of time?
- How can we connect with and confront the masses of young adults and teenagers in our region with God's truth?

I could soon tell that some of my own staff and key leaders were a little nervous just because I was asking these questions. They could smell potential change on the horizon, and they knew that change is never easy. They could sense a passionate restlessness in my spirit. From some people the response was, "Why fix something that isn't broken? We're growing by leaps and bounds. We shouldn't mess with anything. The Devil might try to get in during the process!" For many, our conflict-free environment had become an oasis from previous bad church experiences, but we were still disconnected from the truly unchurched.

Others, however, were simply waiting for my leadership. They understood more than I did that the culture and demographics were quickly changing in our area, but our church was not changing with it. They knew we were becoming more disconnected every day from the very people we were called to reach. From that perspective, the Devil was already in and the real biblical function of the church was already broken!

Peace or Progress

I must admit that up until now Midway's journey had been relatively easy. We just grew. We had a great choir, good Southern gospel music, a well organized Sunday School, and good expository preaching. Every year we grew. We watched for space obstacles, parking obstacles, volunteer obstacles and relationship obstacles. People felt great about inviting their friends to Midway to hear our choir and young pastor, but most of those who came and stayed were people who already knew Christ. Each staff member pretty much did their own planning for the weekends without interacting with one another. We had a weekly staff meeting that revolved mostly around scheduling events. Every staff member was committed to do "their thing" with excellence, but we were working parallel to each other instead of working as a team. No staff member had any opportunity for input or evaluation of another person's area of ministry.

During that time period, I became very transparent and admitted that I didn't have a clue what kind of changes would be required of us, but that God had shown me enough reality that I could not leave things the way they had always been. For me, it was a journey into new territory, and I knew it would be difficult and humbling. I was OK with both of those things spiritually. I knew that without walking by faith it was impossible to please God. I also knew that God loves for us to walk humbly before Him. I knew that not everyone had gone through the process I had during the previous months, and I also knew that some people that I dearly loved would not buy into this new direction. Up until then no full time staff member had left during my entire journey at Midway, but I realized that the challenges that lay ahead would surely push some into areas of ministry change they might not want to go into. The crises and spiritual awareness had been real for me. God had taken me to a whole new understanding of His purpose for the church. I loved Him passionately and I dearly loved the people He had called me to lead. Every crisis demands a response. The question for me was: Do I want complete peace in the church or do I want progress? I realized one must be sacrificed for the other. If I chose peace, the church would ultimately become more inward focused, self-righteous, plateau, and die. If I chose progress, what changes would be required and how and when should I get started?

Chapter 2, part 2 (Marty)

Unexpected Struggle

I never expected to endure the personal ministry crisis that came my way. Believing that expository preaching was about the only thing needed to create a growing church, I was surprised and disappointed when our attendance began to roller coaster—a pattern that lasted about three years.

We had done everything our pastoral staff already knew to do and that had been suggested for us to try. Very early in my tenure, our Sunday School training for teachers and leaders session was attended by more than fifty people; I considered it a great success. The conference covered all the traditional elements of successful Sunday School—assistant teachers, group leaders, inreach leader, outreach leader, and the like. We were organized to the max. This is not to say that there was no fruit; there was. But at the next Sunday School training, we only had about twenty people, maybe less. There was an intrinsic problem that I could not yet identify.

I was convinced that if we just kept at it, things would eventually change. Our pastoral staff read *Revitalizing the Sunday Morning Dinosaur* by Ken Hemphill and we brought out the cardiac paddles to begin the revitalization. It didn't work and my uneasiness continued. I had not yet considered that working harder was not better if we were working harder on the wrong things.

Unfruitful Efforts

At my urging, we instituted an effort to place a Bible in every home within a five-mile radius, an idea that was birthed after having read an article on the Coca-Cola company in which the president's stated goal was to put a Coke into the hand of every person on earth. I thought and said to our people, "If a secular company can have that big a goal, why can't we reach the people around us with an infinitely more important 'product'?"

So, one Saturday a month for several months we loaded our cars with little bags printed with the church logo, containing a Bible and some church literature, and went door-to-door in carefully pre-selected subdivisions around us. Almost everyone was polite, at least, but I began to wonder just how effective we were really being as we knocked on those doors at 9:30 or 10 o'clock on Saturday morning, especially since none of the contacts ever seemed to show up at church. It really hit home one day when a fellow, obviously roused from sleep, answered the door in his bathrobe. When I announced why we were there, there was an audible groan of disgust and I would not have been surprised if he had thrown the entire bag and contents into our faces. As it was, he just slammed the door and, presumably, returned to his slumber.

In all the months and all the hundreds of Bibles distributed, we only had one person ever come to New Bethany as a result. Two of our men spoke with one homeowner who they led in a prayer for salvation. He and his wife came the following day, but never came into the auditorium, remaining instead in the lobby. They never returned. I could not help but think, "Somehow, I don't think it is supposed to work like this."

Our "visitation" program, like most other things that we were doing, trended downward. All the encouragement in the world would only bring a few people out, neither would the free dinner that we began offering prior to our leaving the building to witness to our prospects sustain an increased participation. As I had experienced so often during weekly visitation at my previous church, fewer people were home and others were not prepared for unannounced guests and thus not overly happy to allow us into houses that were unkempt due to busy weekly schedules. Those two examples do not even begin to cover the difficulty with getting childcare on visitation nights. Finally, one of our faithful men responded to my expression of frustration with logic that I knew deep down to be true: "Just because I do not come to 'visitation' does not mean I'm not sharing Christ." Sometimes I tried to comfort my disconcerting feelings by assuring myself that we had done what we were supposed to do and it was not our fault if people were not responding. But the gnawing inside reminded me that we had not done all we could do—we had just done all we could do considering our state of being.

We offered "witness training" classes with the requisite visiting times to try and lead someone to Christ and then report back on our successes. Again, the few that prayed never seemed to make it to a single church service. Another of our pastors and I taught the *Becoming a Contagious Christian* course on a series of Sunday nights, but we did not become viral as a result. I asked for prayer and we prayed. We had a "Prayer and Fasting Calendar" with members agreeing to do one or both at least one day per month. In other words, there was an intentional effort to do all that we knew to do all the while I continued to wonder what was missing.

We changed the name of "Sunday School" to "Small Groups" in hopes that it would communicate a different idea, but, since we still met at 9:30 on Sunday morning, it was very difficult to bring about the genuine sense of biblical community that I believed God wanted us to have. After a year of using the new term verbally and in print, I began to notice some of my most ardent supporters reverting to saying "Sunday School." Even in our pastoral staff meeting we began to charge 25 cents each time one of us said, "Sunday School." It was as if no one could make the vision stick.

At that point a truth was confirmed to me: the vast majority of people who had been raised, as had I, in a traditional church atmosphere were actually unable to hear what was being said about transition. It was not a rebellion; instead, every single new concept and idea was being filtered through a very specific philosophical paradigm of ministry—the one that we refer to as *traditional*. I came to understand that so entrenched was that way of thinking that the only solution that would allow and encourage new thinking was to remove as much of the old structures as we could, so that there was no way to try to place the new wine into old wineskins. I began to pray that we could have new wineskins all the way around.

Eyes Opening

I really was not caught up in a "numbers game," as can be so easily done in our success oriented society and especially in church life. I was caught up in a "we aren't really reaching the lost" awareness. It became increasingly obvious that as the communities around us were exploding in growth, we were only reaching people who were raised in church or had some appreciation of church life. In other words, people just like us.

As we studied demographic data we learned that more than 45,000 people (at that time) within a fifteen minute driving window of our campus attended no church at all.

In order to confirm this data about our community, I turned to my oldest daughter, who worked for Godiva Chocolates at our local mall. I purchased about 50 four-piece boxes of truffles and began my front door interviews. Armed with questions about how churches and Christians were viewed in our community, I began. Unlike surveys I had done before that sought family information, these questions asked for opinions, which almost all Americans are happy to give. Of course, the promise of those truffles did not hurt the cause. I was even able to get men to respond when reminded of how happy their wives would be with them when given these unexpected sweets. These surveys helped solidify my thinking that something was amiss in the way we did church. Those that were already like us were happy to join, while those that were not like us were staying away in droves. It could not be explained with a trite, "Well, the world never has liked the church," because the world was not getting close enough to give it a try! The terminology that we were using was not communicating what we were trying to say.

It was during these days of self-examination and church examination that I often spent time with a pastor from a neighboring church. We prayed together about our churches and our area. We wondered aloud and often if God would ever really visit our churches with His power. We pounded our heads against numerous invisible walls as we struggled through and, alternately, kept each other from complete collapse. Reviewing the great moves of God in history, frankly, did little other than frustrate me at that point. If God could send His Spirit in New England, China and Wales, why not in Buford and Flowery Branch? It felt as if I was part of a cosmic science fair project, surrounded by a maze of walls, not knowing where to go next because every new hallway looked like the dozen or so I had already traversed.

Add to this the already heavy burdens of ministry and almost anyone can see why so few pastors and churches ever attempt to transition. Paul noted in his list of trials, that "above all, [was] the ongoing ministry of the churches," and it is a genuine reality. I'll never forget the one man who brought a book to me, *Transitioning*, by Dan Southerland, former pastor of Flamingo Road Baptist Church in Tampa, Florida. I took it and immediately identified with what he had been through and appreciated what Flamingo Road had attempted to do (and did). Ironically, in a matter of months the man who gave me the book had left the church, never to return, unwilling to support me or our attempted transition.

It was during this period of time that I wondered whether we would ever make a transition ourselves, and how many people would have to enter a Christless eternity before we began to see the urgency of a ministry style that was effective in reaching those who did not know Christ. I heard a statistic that for every one hundred churches that realize a transition is needed, only ten will even try and only two will succeed. My frustration deepened, though I became determined that if we ever attempted such a transition, I would do my very best to lead us to be one of the two.

During this time of crisis, God sent a new friend my way in the form of a former pastor who had left his church under a cloud. I had only known him by reputation, but I had been sure to prejudge him sufficiently. Imagine my utter surprise when he showed up at New Bethany one Sunday and was very gracious to me after the message. A phone call the next day resulted in a lunch meeting at which I said, "I only know you by reputation and I've heard something about you leaving your former church. If you want to talk about it, fine, if not, that's fine, too. I'm going to be your friend either way, because I cannot believe that it's a mistake that God brought you to the church I pastor if He had no intention for us to know one another."

He told of being ostracized by his former friends in ministry. He told me the entire story as well as the stories that had been told of him that were not true; of days and nights spent alone crying out to God when his marriage fell apart; of how he longed to be in ministry and if that meant witnessing to the waitress at lunch then that would be the ministry he would accept.

This friendship deepened, even though he did not seem particularly thrilled with some of the methodology that I advocated and some of the direction that I believed God wanted New Bethany to go. I include this story because he was one of two people who told me to give up and look for another church. "The church will never change," he said. "It's too set in its ways." (In an evidence of God's sense of humor, the second person who told me to give up is the co-author of this book!) But, I could not shake the depth of the impression that God wanted me to try and lead this body to transition, rather than simply leaving for another ministry or planting a new church in our general area.

Another reason I was compelled to lead in this direction was because all of our pastoral staff, some of whom were new since my arriving at New Bethany, believed we must attempt the transition and to not at least attempt it was tantamount to sin. We had spent literally hundreds of hours studying, praying, and weeping over what we wanted to see God do and that we hadn't yet seen. They had counted the cost and were willing to pay whatever price might be necessary.

I've learned that one of the qualities of leadership is that the leader sees before others see, which means the leader often recognizes problems when others are still seeing successes. In our situation this created frustrations for the other people involved when, from all appearances, we were still a good, solid church. Why any need for change and especially any drastic change? What pastors and other leaders recognize is how often a celebration of life is tinged by the aroma of death wafting in from nearby.

At a later time, I alluded to this particular leadership quality in a journal entry that I had written on a personal retreat at the Simpsonwood Center in Norcross, Georgia:

> "I am sitting on a bench watching the morning mist along the Chattahoochee River. The water is flowing steady and strong and I hear the splash of shoals not too distant to my left...but I can't see them from where I am. To see the shoals, I must get up and move.
>
> "The last two or three years at New Bethany have been pretty much the same way. I can 'hear' what God wants our church to be and how He wants us to reach our community and our world, but because I have not gotten up and moved beyond the mist and fog, I have not been able to see it.
>
> "I am on this personal retreat to try and get a handle on what it is God wants us to do; me in particular. My Bible is open to Joshua 1, the text of my first sermon ever preached at New Bethany in 1998. It was on the basis of this 'trial sermon' that I was called as pastor.
>
> "Verses 1-9 have always been favorites of mine and today I saw something, even before I actually read the passage, that I had never seen before. All those times that God was saying 'be strong and courageous,' He was not speaking to the Israelites; He was speaking to their leader, Joshua. There are

twelve statements of affirmation to Joshua concerning his leadership. Why so many? Perhaps God knew what Joshua would face and was preparing him for it. This seems the OT counterpart to the Great Commission. The authority of Christ, the commands of Christ and the assurance of Christ; it's all there.

"Will I listen to God and walk toward what I can hear even though I don't see it yet?

"The wind shifts as I sit beside the river. The 'wild river' smell floats into and opens my nostrils. It could be Panther Creek or it could be Sherwood Creek. There is a smell to wild water flowing free. It's where the power is, where the freedom is—it's where I want to be."

I do not now remember the reason that I initially entered our local LifeWay Christian Store in August of 2002, but it led to an acceleration of a change in me and planted the seed that grew into a new philosophy of ministry that I now believe to be more thoroughly biblical than the model to which I had held. The two books that I purchased that day were *UnLearning Church* by Michael Slaughter, and *An Unstoppable Force* by Erwin McManus. Though Slaughter's volume brimmed with insight and encouragement, it was the second book that gave voice to things inside of me that I did not even know were screaming.

I've read *Unstoppable* so many times now that it's highlighted in yellow, bracketed in red and underlined in blue—if I looked hard enough, I could probably find pencil marks, too. I recommended it to friends. One Christian college prof even adopted it as a text after my recommendation to one of his students. The New Bethany staff of pastors purchased it and read it over a series of weeks, taking breaks to discuss the concepts contained in it.

For the first time, all my thinking, prayer and study was distilled into a theological framework that made sense of my frustration and mind bending thoughts of a missional ecclesiology that began to give me hope. I wondered, "How could I have missed this for so long? And more, how could so many churches be missing this?" It seemed as if there was sense in which many western churches, as the Pharisees of old, had traded the commandments of God for the traditions of men.

Vision

Chapter 3, part 1 (Todd)

Desperation

It's been said that "desperate times call for desperate measures." One hot summer day when I was just a kid, I ran out of the house with socks on my feet, but no shoes. We lived in the country, and going barefooted in the summertime was as common as eating when we were hungry, but it was a little unusual for me to leave my socks on. Why I did it that day, I have no idea. I jumped on my brother's bicycle and headed down our road that ultimately ended at a major state highway with lots of traffic. It was downhill all the way, and extremely fast was the name of the game. I started down the hill that day just as I had done many times before. It was a great experience as I pedaled at breakneck speed.

As I got within sight of the highway, I pressed the cable-operated brake handle only to find that the brakes did not work. I vividly recall the panic and fear that immediately came upon me as I realized I had only two options, and both of them involved pain at the deepest levels. I could continue on the path I was on and roll into the highway, facing probable death; or I could push my sock-covered feet firmly onto the hot pavement until I could slow down enough to ditch the bike. Neither were pleasant options, but at least one of them avoided death. A week later, my socks with holes and scabbed feet were beautiful signs of life.

Now, many years later, I felt like I was back on that bicycle, except this time there were eternal consequences at stake for thousands of people all around me. I felt like the church was pedaling as fast as possible toward certain death, but most churchgoers seemed to be content and enjoying the ride, not realizing what lay ahead. I knew I could continue to keep things the way they had always been, or I could help bring about change that would also involve lots of personal pain during the journey. But at least there was the hope of life.

What If?

I didn't really know how to get started, but one thing was for sure: I needed to clearly see where God wanted us to go. In the midst of my quest to get inside the heart of God concerning the church, I found myself drifting away into a perfect world of "what ifs."

- What if there was a church designed to connect to the 84.6 percent of our county's population who were not actively involved in a church, instead of being designed to connect with the 14.4 percent who were already connected?
- What if there was a church that loved God more that life itself?

- What if there was a church more committed to love other people than to defend man-made laws about their own cultural brand of religion?
- What if there was a church flexible enough culturally to meet people where they are, and biblically and spiritually grounded enough to lead them into a great relationship with Christ?
- What if there was a church that didn't qualify the value of people by the color of their skin, the money in their bank account, the kind or location of their home, their vocation, their choice of political party, or the kind of car they drive?
- What if there was a church that just saw all people as the ones Jesus died for, and considered every other issue secondary for the sake of the gospel?
- What if there was a church that served together year after year without fussing and fighting over nonessential issues, while at the same time aggressively and proactively carrying out the Great Commission with joy and effectiveness?
- What if there was a church that taught and explained—clearly and unapologetically—foundational doctrines in which the Bible is clear, while remaining gracious and kind in areas that are not clear in Scripture.
- What if there was a church that generously gave their time and resources to build the kingdom of God with excellence around the world?

The Church God Dreams About

I felt almost as if I was starting in ministry all over again. It was simple and raw. I began studying Scripture with new eyes beginning with several key passages regarding the church (Matt. 16:17-19; Acts 1-8, 11-13; Eph. 5:22-33; Rev. 2-3). So much of what I believed about the church had been developed as a result of the culture I grew up in and the churches of which I had been a part. In addition to being ineffective, to me it seemed like "church life" had become extremely complex and busy. I knew, at some point, I would read the works and studies of other men, but foundationally, I wanted to take a fresh new look at what God had to say.

At the very beginning of this new journey, the words of Jesus from Matthew 16:17-19 began to ring loudly in my spirit. "You are Peter, and on this rock I will build My church and the gates of Hades will not prevail against it." It had been a statement of instruction and conviction to His disciples that—on the surface—seems almost out of context. The statements before and after it have been a source of controversy and theological debate for centuries. Was Peter to be the foundation of the church? If so does that mean that Peter was the first pope? Was Jesus referring to Himself as the BIG rock and to Peter as a little rock, and stating that He would build the church upon Himself? Was He simply doing a word play from the Greek language of the day? Was He referring to Peter's leadership for the future direction of the church and his prominent role on launch day for the church at Pentecost?

Then there's the "keys to the kingdom" discussion that follows. What were the keys? Who exactly did He give them to? What did He mean by "bind" and "loose"?

Then there's the broader context that this whole discussion immediately follows a warning about the teachings of the Pharisees and a question about Jesus' own identity. Personally I had begun to realize that my own attitudes about life and people were much closer to those of the Pharisees than those of Jesus. It was eye-opening and humbling to realize I was now a recovering Pharisee!

I wondered if those attitudes had perhaps hidden the true identity of Jesus from those I was called to reach? Had the entire church evolved into a people that were more concerned with "their" brand of religion than demonstrating the love of Jesus to the people who needed Him most?

There sometimes seemed to be more questions than answers, but in the midst of it all, Jesus had made a decree. He said, "I will build MY CHURCH and the gates of hell will not prevail against it." In that statement, I saw three things that rang loud and clear.

First of all was the fact that He would do the building. He did not necessarily exclude our involvement. As a matter of fact, we learn in Ephesians 4:7-16 that He would build His church by divinely calling and gifting people, as He chooses, to serve in His kingdom. When this is done "according to the effective working by which every part does its share, causes growth of the body for the edifying of itself in love" (v. 16). This teaching seemed to paint a beautiful picture of a team of people working together, each serving in the positions for which they have been divinely gifted and called. As they serve with excellence, the body of Christ grows and becomes more effective at building the kingdom of God.

Secondly, He declared that He would build HIS CHURCH. The church is often referred to as HIS bride and there is always a sense of ownership and possessiveness in such a relationship. I had to wonder if the church concept had been somewhat stolen from Him and turned into something not quite as glorious as intended. I certainly didn't want to be guilty of that in my own journey, in the past or the future.

Thirdly, He stated as a matter of fact that "the gates of Hades would not prevail against it." This statement perhaps caused me more consternation than any of the others. With thousands of local churches in America remaining small and ineffective year after year, and a decreasing number of people influenced by the church's message with each generation; too often it seemed like the forces of hell were winning. The constant bombardment of negative information regarding the church certainly painted a bleak picture. Church splits, denominational politics, immorality of church leaders, financial scandals, blatant racism in the church, a constant emphasis upon wealth and extravagance, and the refusal of different evangelical groups to work together—all this shows signs of a church that is, at best, self-centered and severely sick.

Church Gone Wrong

I had even seen my own home church experience a major split at one point. During that time period people felt confused, disappointed and defeated. There were several issues involved that caused the big blow-up, but one of them involved my brother and me and several others in our youth group. I was twelve or thirteen years old. We had raised money for the youth group to go on a trip to Disney. Through a series of discussions one night after we arrived in Orlando, our volunteer youth director bought vodka for anyone who wanted it and several of us got so drunk we couldn't walk. It was our little secret for a few months, but sometime later the youth director was nominated to be a deacon. The night of youth drunkenness under his leadership was soon exposed and a series of controversial "special called" business meetings and dissension ensued over the next couple of years. Looking back, I'm reminded that those in the church, attendees and leaders alike, often do foolish things, and if not handled very wisely and submissively from everyone involved, they can be the downfall of a great fellowship of people.

I remember one particular "special called" business meeting that more resembled a union hall meeting than a church gathering. Right in the middle of the meeting, a sweet lady stood to ask a question. At that very moment, my childhood friend, a dog named Banjer, walked into the church and down the aisle. Banjer was perhaps the best friend I ever had. He had saved my life when I was just a toddler and had been hit by a car at one point, leaving him with only three good legs. The pastor had a perfect view down the center aisle and could clearly see him from the pulpit. When this dear lady stood to ask her question, the pastor, distracted by the animal, said, "Would somebody please get that dog out of the church?" A man on the other side of the church, who didn't know Banjer was in the building, jumped up in anger and in southern slang demanded, "Don't you call her no dog!"

That event may seem hilarious these many years later, but at the time there was little that resembled the church that Jesus said He would build. It's just one more example of how easily the church can become deceived and distracted from the real mission of the church. As I pondered all of these things, it was increasingly evident to me that the church desperately needed help. It seemed it was already on life support, and now the life support machine was beginning to break down!

The Way It Ought to Be

After meditating on Jesus' words in Matthew, I turned to the book of Acts. It was there that I saw a real movement of God. The church wasn't all about a "place" called the church. It was all about a people whose lives had been radically transformed by the power of God. Thousands of people came to know Christ, were baptized and continued with a sense of "togetherness." Over and over again, I saw the words "together" and in "one accord."

As I studied the movements and patterns of the early church, I was impressed with their love and sacrifice for one another and their obvious commitment to be the people of God every day. They didn't simply "go" to church. They "were" the church. God was doing His mission through His people every day; within a couple of years, thousands were coming into God's kingdom as a result. HE was indeed building HIS church. As persecution came and imprisonment followed, Peter proved himself a committed leader when he declared, "We must obey God rather than men!" (Acts 5:29) Continued persecution led many of them to leave Jerusalem and go to the regions of Judea and Samaria. Even one of their persecutors, a Pharisee named Saul, soon came to Christ and passionately preached the gospel in the very synagogues he had previously taught in as a Pharisee. Peter also stepped into new territory as he overcame personal cultural barriers to preach the gospel to the Gentile family of Cornelius. As a result, Cornelius and his entire household came to experience the beautiful grace of God.

Then there was the church at Antioch, mentioned in Acts 11-13. It was established partly as a result of the persecution and stoning of Stephen. It was among the church at Antioch that masses of Jewish and Gentile people alike would come to experience the grace of God and for the first time in history, a group of people would be called "Christians." In that church, the walls of culture would take a "back seat" to the real mission of the church. From that group of people, missionaries would be intentionally sent to the different races and cultures of the day, to explain and demonstrate the message of Jesus Christ.

It was refreshing to realize that it was to the people of Antioch, who passionately and courageously followed the heart of God, that I owed my spiritual heritage. It was only through a few risk-takers, once again committed to "obey God rather than men," that the gospel had ultimately made it to my ancestors in Scotland and Ireland hundreds of years later. This study led me to ask a series of questions? Could it be that every step of my own spiritual journey, and those of the church I now led, carried with them some sense of personal connection to the generations that would follow? I asked myself, "Would there someday be people around the world who would link their spiritual heritage to our willingness to take such risks as the early church?" If so, I knew I would have to be a greater risk-taker than I had ever been, and I was again reminded that pain would probably be involved.

Images were beginning to emerge in my mind of a people who, if willing to change, could change the future for thousands of people. Jesus had prayed and taught His disciples to pray, "Our Father ... Your kingdom come. Your will be done on earth as it is in heaven." He had told his followers to go into *all* of the world and make disciples, yet most churches in America remained a single homogeneous group, safely segregated from the rest of society. To me it was obvious that God wanted His kingdom, and a touch of heaven, to come to earth. The church was to play a major role in that process. The church at its best could help every heart and every home experience a touch of heaven. However, in order to fulfill that dream, I knew we had to become culturally connected to the people we were called to reach. It would be a difficult journey, because for most of my life I had attempted to stay disconnected and isolated from the people around me who were not like me. In turn, the churches I led enjoyed a sense of spiritual and cultural safety as I regularly preached to isolate the cultures around us and to "reaffirm" our own distinctiveness.

Change Required

As I contemplated the real challenges that were ahead, I sensed God leading me to make changes that would affect both the weekly gatherings of people at Midway and our attitude toward the people around us on a day-to-day basis. Our weekly gatherings needed to be joyful, celebrative and inviting. They already were to some people, but our immediate area had become more culturally diverse and we had made little attempt to connect. Our music was geared to connect culturally toward those who were lifelong churchgoers from the West Georgia area, usually above the age of 45. The music was done with excellence, but it was one more way of being culturally disconnected from the changing population around us.

Every encounter throughout the week needed to be seen as a divine appointment to somehow bring Jesus to the surface of life. We would need to, intentionally, find areas of need in our community and attempt to be the eyes, ears, heart, and hands of Jesus. We would need to personally get to know many people that our cultures had taught us to be afraid of and to avoid. On the outside, Midway would attempt to be a people who take the love and message of Christ to the people across the street and around the world. On the inside, Midway would attempt to become a place where people could *begin*, *belong* and *become* all they could be.

I knew the journey ahead would be difficult and painful. I knew I would receive criticism and resistance from some of my closest ministry companions and fellow pastors. There was a time when I had done the criticizing. I fully understood their concerns and points of view. However, I also knew that 85.6 percent of people in our area were not connected to a church on a weekly basis. I knew that with every passing generation the life-transforming message of Jesus Christ was being embraced by fewer and fewer people. For years I had been speaking on behalf of those inside the four walls of the church. I quickly defended everything we did, all the while being unaware that the facts showed the church was heading toward probable death. Now I felt like God was calling me to speak on behalf of those on the outside. It was new territory for me and I knew the potential disasters that could erupt from going down this path, but "What If..."?

Chapter 3, part 2 (Marty)

"No longer can any one community of Christ's followers dictate what another church must to do to

succeed. I'm 'unlearning' the model of cloning someone else's blueprint. That era is over. God's kingdom is not best represented by franchises of McChurch."[1]

Michael Slaughter

Learning

My personal studies had unleashed a torrent of new thoughts within my understanding of God's purpose and plan, creating a continuous hunger for what the church could and should be. I read Bill Hybels' fond recollection of the challenge that stirred him as he listened to the passion of Dr. Gilbert Belzekian, when referring to the early church of Acts 2:

> "There once was a community of believers who were so totally devoted to God that their life together was charged with the Spirit's power.
> "In that band of Christ followers, believers loved each other with a radical kind of love...They laughed and cried and prayed and sang and served together in authentic Christian fellowship."[2]

My own heart was stirred when Hybels, at the Willow Creek Leadership Summit in 2003 repeated over and again, "I believe that the local church is the hope of the world."

As I studied scripture regarding the call of Abraham, the responsibility of the nation of Israel (which they carelessly frittered away), the incarnation and life of Christ, and the early church, I became convinced that something was

---

[1]- Michael Slaughter, *UnLearning Church* (Group: Loveland, OH), 15.
[2]- Bill Hybels, *Courageous Leadership* (Zondervan: Grand Rapids), 17.

missing in our church, the church in the North American context and the West in general. A new word entered into my vocabulary: *missional*.[3] With a growing hunger I began to gain clarity about partnering with God in the *missio dei*, the "mission of God." The philosophical ropes of the traditional style of ministry began to loosen their hold and a more biblical understanding began to make its way into my mind.

I gained understanding of being a "sent people" from a "sending God" and that mission was a part of the nature of God just as surely as righteousness and holiness are. This DNA is replicated in the people of God, yet has been suppressed by materialism or separated out as an optional activity. I remembered Jesus' words, "As the Father has sent me, I also send you" (John 20:21). These words do not simply refer to the fact of being sent, but to the fashion of the sending, ie, an incarnational approach to mission.

A new vision began to be birthed in me, a vision that did not depend on having two thousand people in the same place each Sunday. It might mean that more people were being sent out via church planting or that we encouraged our best people to international mission status. I wanted to see disciples living in community more than just increasing numbers of people attending, while they continued to live individualistically. I longed to see deepening friendships and authentic Christian fellowship in the gospel of Jesus instead of

[3]- The word "missional" is believed to have been first used by Dr. Francis DuBuose in his 1983 work, *God Who Sends*. Of late its usage has regained notice through such people as Darrell Guder and The Gospel and Our Culture Network.

around college football.

I did not long for a transition in our church just to be trying something different, but as the fruition of a vision to be a more biblical church--a church reborn with a missional ecclesiology. It was imperative that we break loose from the box of "doing church" to gain the freedom to "be the church." As Craig van Gelder, in *The Essence of the Church*, writes:

> "The church lives within the context of culture and is, therefore, always contextual. Jesus demonstrated the importance of contextualization in the incarnation. Just as the Word became flesh, so also the church is enfleshed in human cultures as the body of Christ. The church being enfleshed within culture means that the church by nature is to be contextual in every particular setting in which it exists. It has the inherent capacity to fit into every culture, to be relevant within the organizational and institutional dimensions of any context."[4]

I came to realize that my confusion of the culture and the world was the major contributing factor to my misunderstanding the nature of the church. It had been beyond me to reconcile the entire idea of "being in the world, but not of the world."

God at Work

To assist me through this learning, God providentially brought a series of conferences across my path. Because of my heritage, virtually every conference I had attended as a

[4]- Craig Van Gelder, *The Essence of the Church* (Baker Books: Grand Rapids), 119.

pastor had been hosted by my denomination or a church affiliated with my denomination. (After all, since we were right about everything, why go anywhere else?) These new conferences, however, were enlightening for me. Who would have thought that pastors from a large cross-section of denominations were struggling with the same things that were bothering me? These conferences, sponsored by a nondenominational, conservative seminary were hosted at various churches across America: The Community Church of Joy (Evangelical Lutheran) outside Phoenix, Arizona, Willow Creek Community Church, South Barrington, Illinois, The Church of the Resurrection (Methodist), Kansas City, Kansas, and others. I was hearing from speakers like George G. Hunter, Warren Bird, Steve Sjogren, Don Wilson and Dale Galloway. And, while not in agreement with every theological jot and tittle, I could tell that there was an understanding of the church and its mission that had eluded me until this point.

Via this conference interaction, it became clear just how much American Christianity had become a sub-culture in which I had happily participated. Though thrilled by the stories of "redemptive analogies" from the jungle memoirs of missionary-authors Don Richardson (*Peace Child, Lords of the Earth* and *Eternity in Their Hearts*) and Bruce Olsen (*Bruchko*), I had failed to connect this to living in the post-Christian (or pre-Christian) culture around me. Merrily we sailed along on the Ship of Zion safely insulated from the world around us that needed saving.

Tim Wright has addressed the issue of God and culture well. In *The Prodigal Hugging Church*, he says:

> "God's strategy for reaching culture is absolutely astounding: God, in the person of Jesus, decided to become like culture. He became like the people he wants to find-so that he can put his arms around them, affirm them, welcome them, and ultimately lead them home."[5]

Erwin McManus nails the indictment to the front door of each and every church when he writes,

> "The diminishing influence of the American church on American society is not simply because fewer people are going to church, but *fewer people are going to church because of the diminishing influence of Christ on the church itself."* [Emphasis mine.][6]

And, nowhere is His waning influence on His own church seen anymore clearly than the "bunker mentality" that most churches have toward the lost.

When did the church become our refuge from the world? How did it happen the church became the place that we went when trying to get away from those we are supposed to be trying to reach? How did we ever become convinced of the truth of such an anti-biblical expectation that lost people remain lost because they will not come to church, rather than remaining lost because followers of Christ refuse to live the gospel while sharing the gospel them?

Deep down, I knew that the answer was not to simply

---

[5]- Tim Wright, *The Prodigal Hugging Church* (Augsburg Fortress Publishers: Minneapolis), 17.

[6]- Erwin McManus, *An Unstoppable Force* (Group: Loveland, OH), 28.

find a "model" of doing church and copy it. It was more even than transferring the principles that would "work in our situation." We had to be the church that God was calling us to be in our context and in our time. This was a huge deal as our church had just turned 125 years old and had a strong heritage of which many were proud. In addition, we were in an area that was itself transitioning rapidly from rural to suburban, from a place of family farms to street after street of new subdivisions. What I longed for was a body of believers that was biblically sound and culturally authentic; I was not looking to emasculate the scripture through compromise, but to apply what it actually says rather than the legalistic interpretations that I had favored. I hoped that we might come to reject the misinterpretations we had firmly held.

When I heard that the reason that most people do not want to go to church is because they have already been, my vision was a church that would change those expectations. Though I could not, at that time, do anything about the very traditional external appearance of our facilities, I could begin to think about what they experienced when the entered those facilities. New people could be greeting with genuine warmth, a cup of coffee, hot chocolate or tea, they could hear music that bridged a gap to where they were instead of music that reaffirmed their worst fears about church or, still worse, erected yet another wall to a clear hearing and understanding of the gospel; in other words, they could decide within the first few minutes to return rather than to leave and never come back.

A Theology of Change

A study of the early church did much to help me grasp how our church could relate to our culture and engage it with the gospel. The book of Acts chapter 15 records the church council held by the apostles and elders of the Jerusalem church with Paul and Barnabas. Convened for the scandalous purpose of determining whether or not the Gentiles might also be recipients of eternal life, the question hinged on whether or not they would be required to accept specifically Jewish cultural forms before they could be saved. There were some Pharisees who were adamant that, "It is necessary to circumcise them and to command them to keep the law of Moses" (v. 5). In other words, these teachers were arguing, the Gentiles had to become Jews before they could become Christians!

After hearing from Paul and Barnabas that God was saving Gentiles in many places, Peter stood and affirmed this work of God, likening the "Judaizing" to "placing a yoke on the neck of the disciples that neither our fathers nor we have been able to bear" (v. 10). James then referred to an ancient prophecy (Amos 9:11, 12) that assured the calling from the Gentiles a people for God's name. The consensus was that, yes, God was saving Gentiles and, no, they did not first have to adhere to Jewish customs or laws before becoming believers.

The time had come to communicate back to the Gentile believers what the leaders of the Jerusalem church had decided. It was the opportunity of a lifetime to place every necessary restriction on this new wing of the church, as it would soon outstrip its Jewish counterpart in both size and influence. Surely there would be a long list of restrictions-a thorough list of "do's and don'ts" that would be passed through history. I was shocked to find, in the official letter to the Gentile believers, a mere four items of guidance: First, abstain from what has been sacrificed to idols. Second, abstain from eating blood. Next, abstain from meat that has been strangled. Fourth, and last, abstain from sexual immorality.

What?! No restrictions on music? No restrictions on clothes? No restrictions on whether to sit or stand when teaching? On whether to use a pulpit, a stand or stool? Nothing. God intentionally built the flexibility into the church that it needed to flesh out the body of Christ in each and every culture. Missiologist George G. Hunter, in a profile of the early Christian movement, said, "[It] assumed that 'lost people' matter to God, even barbarian people, and need to be found, so reaching them is the Church's main business," adding, "Following the Jerusalem Council, the Movement became culturally relevant."[7] This scriptural truth energized me as to what God might do through our church if we actually began to engage our culture as part of the culture, not as outsiders throwing stones at it.

[7]- From my personal notes of a lecture given by George Hunter in Chicago, IL, October 21, 2003.

As noted by Tim Wright above, the pinnacle of what God thought of culture was demonstrated at the incarnation. Drawing from the life of Christ and the parable of the prodigal son, Wright challenges the local representations of the body of Christ to be "prodigal hugging churches." It was a challenge to me as well.

For a couple of years I had frequented the same Chili's restaurant. Employed there was an exceptional server named Lyndsi. When dining there for lunch, I would always ask to be seated in her area and if I were dining with someone, I would always introduce her as, "Lyndsi, the best server anywhere." It provided openings for infrequent opportunities for sharing the gospel and she was always responsive.

One day I stopped for lunch and asked to be seated in her area only to be informed that she was now working at the bar. I remember standing beside the greeter with my mind running in a thousand directions, trying to decide what I should do. Of course, the number one question for me-my primary mental objection-was, "What if a church member sees me at the bar? What would they think?" I sat in another booth and settled for a different server in the regular part of the restaurant.

Before long, I was swimming in guilt. I simply could not reconcile my behavior with that of Christ's. He frequently and openly dined with "sinners" so much so that He became known as one who was their friend (Luke 6:34). I wrestled with what I should do if again faced with that opportunity.

A couple of weeks later, I fought back tears as I shared that particular incident with our church. Trying to impress upon us the importance of loving people where they are, as they are, I relayed this failure of mine to live that way. I informed those gathered believers that if they were ever to enter an eating establishment and see me sitting at the bar, that they should just assume that I was doing as Jesus did in building a redemptive relationship with someone.

Much to my surprise and gratitude, these Jesus following believers were very receptive and some of them cried as well. Following the service a faithful man came to me and said, "Marty, if it had been two years ago and you had sat down at a bar, you might have been sitting next to me! I think you ought to do as the Lord is leading you."

Deep in my heart I wanted nothing less than a church that loved the way that Jesus did, that related to people the way that Jesus did and was fine with risking reputation, life and limb to see Him glorified in us. Leading them on that journey, though, would prove to be a great challenge of its own-for me and for them.

Change in the Air

Chapter 4, part 1 - (Todd)

Getting Ready

A new vision of what the church could and should be had been firmly planted within me. I had a fresh sense of divine purpose, personal brokenness, repentance, and humility as I stared at the task ahead. For many years, I had believed the church was the hope for the world. Now I believed there was actually hope for the church! The future for thousands of unchurched families in our area could be one of hope if the church could just get its act together and become effective.

In some ways I felt as if God was asking me to get out of the boat and walk on water with Peter; get into the lion's den with Daniel; or into the fire with Shadrach, Meshach, and Abednego. He was taking me way out of my comfort zone, but everything within me said I had to do it or I would be disobedient to the God who had created me for His purposes. I also felt there were men, women, boys and girls whose future rested in the hands of the church's effectiveness.

Preparing the Team

In order to prepare for the journey ahead, I first began to lead our staff through a weekly study on the subject of teamwork. Each week we read one chapter of *The 17 Indispensable Laws of Teamwork*, by John Maxwell. Then we came together and watched a video of John teaching on the same subject, followed by group discussion and prayer for the team. We learned that teamwork would require consistent interaction and communication between the different leaders of each ministry department. In the future, each ministry leader would need to be open for critique from others on the team. In some cases, team members might be asked to move into a new area of ministry or share responsibilities with someone else.

I was very clear that we were going into new territory and that we would never survive if we did not work together as a team. I was not completely sure as to what the future looked like, but as a staff, we were going down this journey together. I shared my love and respect for each of them while I also acknowledged that some of them might not want to go on this journey with me. That would be OK, but every person must commit to work together as a team or they would no longer be on it. Nobody was indispensable, including me.

The journey was not about any one person on our staff or leadership team. It was all about the vision and heart of God to redeem mankind from the curse of sin. It was all about the church becoming effective to reach the thousands of unchurched people all around us, instead of snuggling safely in our corner of the world. More than eighty-five percent of the people in our area were not being impacted by the message of the church on a weekly basis, and the vast majority of those who did attend were over the age of fifty. If some major transformations did not occur, the Christian movement of America would soon become a relic, much like a Model T Ford. Everyone would speak about the "good ole days." They would soon look at the church with nostalgic emotions. They would speak about what she used to be and how their parents and grandparents used to go every week. They would speak about the movements of God in the past. However, for them, there would be little, if any desire to find a place in their own busy schedules for such a life. It was a statistical fact that churchgoers as a whole were not effectively passing on a spiritual heritage to their own children and grandchildren, much less effectively reaching the masses of unchurched.

Dreaming Out Loud—Round One

One of the most important parts of my new journey was how well I could communicate this vision to the church body as a whole. I understood the fact that vision has a tendency to decrease in clarity and passion as it filters through the ranks of an organization. I knew I needed to communicate it in a way that the people could both see it and feel it, and I needed some help in order to do it right. My passion from this new movement of God in my life was obvious in my weekly sermons. I studied and preached with a new sense of urgency. Each week I exposed our church to small portions of what I was learning, somehow hoping the right changes would automatically happen. But they didn't. I soon realized I would have to establish a special time to focus only on our vision for the future. The date was set for Sunday night, September 28, 2003. I called it simply, "Vision Night 2003."

In order to prepare for the big event, I read *Courageous Leadership*, by Bill Hybels, and once again was stretched in my understanding of what the church could be with the right leadership. I saw the importance of using stories of life-change and word pictures to communicate the vision effectively. I read *Developing a Vision for Ministry in the 21st Century*, by Aubrey Malphurs and received immense help to develop the main structure of the vision. Then, for the first time in my life, I read Dr. Martin Luther King's "I have a dream" speech in its entirety. I must admit that I wept before I could get to the end. I felt the real pain of racism that existed in an otherwise modern society. I was reminded that instead of leading the way, the church had perhaps made the least progress of any organization in America since the famous speech had been delivered.

Those three resources assisted me in the development of how the vision for Midway could and should be communicated. I certainly do not compare the quality of my first new vision communication piece I produced to that of these great leaders and communicators, but I did use similar word patterns, pictures, phrases and structure. I read the vision speech given by Bill Hybels to Willow Creek Community Church in 1996 and printed in the Appendix of Aubrey Malphurs' book on developing a vision. I admit that some entire segments of that speech made their way into the communication piece I later developed. Each one of these tools, along with years of study, had their own unique contribution to the development of my new vision and how I was to communicate it.

A part of me naively believed that if I communicated the vision effectively, everyone would jump on board with me and make it their goal to become a part of the solution. It was great to dream, but there was a more realistic part of me that knew it wouldn't be quite that simple. However, above and beyond technique, I wanted to go through the journey with integrity. At one point I met with our deacons to help them understand that if they did not want to go with me to lead the church down this new path, I would still love them and respect them. They were awesome men. Many of them were like family. I had no desire to start over again in a new ministry. However, I was willing to resign and pursue this new vision somewhere else if necessary. I could not deny this new movement of God in my life. I was a different pastor than the one who had arrived at Midway in 1996. I knew I would need to "un-do" many attitudes and philosophies of ministry that I had previously affirmed or put into place. I assured the deacons that the transition would not be easy, but that the alternative was the death and ineffectiveness of the church. Every one of them affirmed that they believed I was to continue as the church's leader, and that they wanted us to continue on our journey together.

So, with a sense of awe and anticipation I gave my Vision Night speech to a large, excited crowd. But to my disappointment and frustration, little real change in attitude and effectiveness followed in the months ahead. However, two great things were accomplished through all of our efforts that night. First of all, it was clear that the future would demand even more from us—flexibility, money, creative thinking—than in the past. Second, knowing what we knew about our community's lost condition, we would not be in neutral in the future. By having this event, I had made a statement about our future. We could not and would not be in love with mediocrity. God had given His best for us, and in return, absolute excellence would be required of us. Too much was at stake to do any less.

Over the following weeks and months, we made some minor changes in staff structure and music. For a few in the congregation, it must have seemed like we had denied the Trinity. Some people who had previously loved me dearly all of a sudden seemed to be a little distant and uncomfortable in my presence. However, I made special efforts to love them and stay connected. I wanted to take as many people as possible on the journey with me.

Dreaming Out Loud—Round Two

The following year, I was confronted with the statistics from Thom Rainer's research that I referred to in a previous chapter. If I had any doubts about this new journey up until now, they went out the window when I saw a solidly steady decline of Christianity with each passing generation. In August 2004 I organized a banquet for about two hundred of our church's key leaders, so I could share this information. In some ways, it was a continuation of the Vision Night 2003 speech, but this time I had even more evidence that the church desperately needed a transformation.

As I gave the declining percentage of believers in each age group, I could hear the groans of some in the room who were as shocked as I was when I first saw them. I asked for their commitment, young and old, to join with me to reach the next generation. Everyone in the room agreed. However, not everyone, including me, knew the changes that would be required for us to become effective. We had no idea how high the walls actually were that separated the unchurched on the outside from the grace of God on the inside. But we had committed to go down the path together.

In the weeks ahead, I continued to introduce new concepts to those on the inside of the church, and new outreach ministries to those on the outside of the church. However, during the following year we grew by a smaller growth rate than any year previously on our journey together. Over the course of six years our growth rate had actually declined from thirty-two percent to six percent. Sometimes I'm a little bit slow, but it was at that point that I realized we were only one year away from being "flat-lined" as an organization.

I now had another major motivating factors with which to reckon. Not only were thousands of people who desperately needed to be reached disconnected from the church, but now Midway was on the verge of moving into maintenance mode. The trend was clear. We had grown for nine years straight, but we were just one year away from joining the thousands of plateaued or declining churches in America. I knew that if we came to a halt, it would be very difficult to get going again, and even more difficult to reach the unchurched. My experience told me that once a church plateaus, the people typically turn more inward in their focus than ever. The fact was that we had just about reached all of the frustrated, disappointed or disgruntled church members and "new move-ins" in our area. If we were going to change the solid downward growth trend, we had no choice but to make a priority out of the more than eighty-five percent of our community who were unchurched. I knew our current church culture was not connecting with those who needed Jesus the most. Just as God meets us where we are, we would have to learn how to do the same for the unchurched.

Dreaming Out Loud – Round Three

In June 2005 as I approached the beginning of my tenth year at Midway, I knew we needed to approach the future with greater vision, passion and intensity than ever before. So in September, I organized an offsite retreat we called "The 10/10 Vision Summit." It was a time when we would evaluate our previous ten years together and dream about our next ten years together.

As we began, I shared the highlights of our journey together up to that point. In humble gratitude, we thanked God for His good hand upon us. We asked for His wisdom and anointing; that He would use us to be a greater tool to build His kingdom in the future than in the past. I then reminded everyone about the percentage of unchurched people living around our church. I reminded them about the declining number of believers in each new generation. I reminded them about Midway's declining growth rate and that if the trend continued, we were only one year away from the danger zone. Finally, the stage was set for us to dream about the next ten years together. We dreamed of potential ways and ministries that might help us become more effective in the future. We dreamed of potential "growth engines" that could help us become effective at reaching unchurched people. It was a concept I had heard Bill Hybels speak of and it just made sense. I could track the different growth cycles of the past, and could clearly see what the "growth engines" were that helped us grow at each point. But times had changed. Our community had changed. I knew we also had to change. The only other alternative was death!

The 10/10 Vision Summit included more than seventy of our leaders. We included representatives from every major ministry, age group, and race in the church. We organized them into ten groups of seven. The staff was there to serve the tables with snacks and water and to collect the information at the end of each session. We hired a professional outsider to lead the event, and no paid staff member was allowed to be a part of any think-tank table. I didn't want to manipulate the thinking of this group. We needed the best creative thinking from every person present, and I wanted to see what God was saying to the group at large. We sought God to guide us in all of our processes.

By the end of the first day, we had a creative-thinking exercise that produced a combined list of more than nine hundred ideas and initiatives. I had never seen a group of people so energized and focused on finding solutions. There was a real sense that God was doing something big in our presence. There were times that I got goose bumps and misty eyes just watching it all unfold. The next day our task was to narrow those nine hundred ideas down to ten new key initiatives or areas where we needed great improvement. The result was the following list:

1. Home Teams
2. Saturday Night Worship
3. Sports/Wellness/Recreation Ministry
4. Lifestyle Workshops
5. Mentoring for Students/Children
6. External Marketing/Communication
7. Community Partnerships
8. Multicultural Ministries
9. Coffee House/Satellite Services
10. Internal Communication

On the final night, each group had to develop a drama about their key initiative and act it out in front of the entire group. It was an awesome experience, as each participant took to heart developing a new way of connecting to the unchurched. The creativity in the room was again astounding. During the drama time, every emotion seemed to reach its peak. One person who was acting out the part of a hurting family member in one of our proposed community partnerships was supposed to pretend to weep. But as they entered the role playing their acting turned into real weeping as they felt the pain of someone in need. Finally, the vision was becoming real in the hearts of those who could help lead it to become a reality. The next morning we rated each new initiative with levels of priority and urgency and reported our initiatives to the church body the next weekend.

From Dream to Reality

As I look back, it was the 10/10 Vision Summit that finally helped me clearly and effectively communicate the vision that had burned within me with such intensity. God was saying some of the same things to those leaders at the Summit that He had been saying to me in my own spirit. Every key initiative had come from the heart of someone who wasn't a paid staff member. Some of them were even much more passionate about some of the initiatives than I had ever been. There was some on the list that had never come to my mind. Once again I was reminded that they were simply waiting for my leadership. Some of these initiatives could be implemented in some form within a few weeks, while others would require years. All of them would require change.

However, just the smell of change caused some to question the entire process of the Summit before we even left to return home. However, it was obvious that God was doing something awesome and great in our midst. The ship, so to speak, had finally left the dock and the winds of the Spirit of God had filled the sail. I was more convinced than ever that God was at the helm.

It had been over two years since I had driven home from South Georgia with a holy dissatisfaction after being confronted with the statistics about the unchurched in our area. Now, God had moved in the hearts of many others who could help lead the journey. It was time to act. Every detail of our ministry would need to be looked at in light of the vision God had given us. Our vision would still need to be refined and packaged. It would need to be simple, and easy to grasp and explain. Our new initiatives would need to be implemented. New obstacles would have to be managed. Our communication would have to be at its best. Each staff member and church member would have to decide if they wanted to invest in and be a part of this new vision. I was fully aware that there were many challenges ahead, but I was glad to be on the ship that had just left the dock.

Chapter 4, part 2 (Marty)

"The church culture in North America is a vestige of the original movement, an institutional expression of religion that is in part a civil religion and in part a club where religious people can hang out with other people whose politics, worldview and lifestyle match theirs."[1]

Reggie McNeal

Change in the Air

Around the middle of 2002 I came to the conclusion that God's plan was for me to attempt to lead New Bethany through a transitional period that would result in, as Todd and I have now stated it, "a biblically faithful body that connects culturally, influences locally and extends globally." I knew that there was no guarantee that this attempt would be successful and, frankly, no guarantee that I would not be fired or asked to leave. While I understood that possibility, the belief that God was going to accomplish this gave me hope that however dark the valley, we would come out on the other side.

New Bethany had already undergone some transitioning with varying degrees of success. Our music ministry transitioned from a very traditional piano, organ and many older hymns to a full band with mostly newer songs. Though we were not a rock concert every Sunday it was decidedly more upbeat than before and more than a little

[1]- McNeal, 1.

louder. This was pleasing to some and displeasing to some. Some people had left New Bethany primarily due to this change; others had come because of it.

We had continued one transition that had already begun before my arrival and answered the question: Who actually is responsible to lead the church under the leadership of Christ? Is it the senior pastor, the pastors, the deacons or another group? Although our deacon body had relinquished their "power" prior to my being called, and announced their willingness to serve with the pastors and to serve them when needed, many deacons' meetings still became the second coming of the Building and Grounds Committee.

Leadership from our then-chairman of deacons, given at a critical time, changed the direction of the deacon ministry to a full servant oriented body. They currently minister to our widows and widowers, providing an invaluable ministry to this sometimes neglected part of the body. There were a few members still hung onto the idea that the role of deacon is to "straighten out the pastor," but the majority of members took to heart the Acts 6 pattern and supported the pastors as Christ's leaders of the body and the deacons as His servants to it.

After these transitions, I realized that the others that we needed to make were not going to be pieces of cake either. In fact, the toughest ones were yet to come. Some of these would try me while at least one had the inherent potential to split the church.

I began to preach, as often as the text would allow, on ecclesiology, the doctrine of the church. Through much study and the wisdom of others I gained understanding that mission is part of the DNA of the church, not just a function that fits alongside the children's choir, visitation and the fellowship committee. As I began to understand more and more of God's nature, I taught on the missionary nature of God-that sending is actually part of God's nature. We studied that the building is not the "house of God," but that the believers are. People needed to grasp what Scripture actually taught about the church and its responsibility in the world. For that to occur, a missional ecclesiology needed to be developed.

My first training effort was on Sunday nights following the evening service. I invited all the leaders and potential leaders of the church to meet with the deacons and me on the first Sunday evening of each month. Invitees were strategic and I made sure that there were some from every demographic of the body. I spent about 30-40 minutes teaching the entire group and, when finished, we had deacons' meeting. To coincide with my talks I provided fill-in-the-blank style note sheets so as to gain the most memory impact from each session. We talked about culture, the church, music, dress, mission, God, the Bible and more. Everything was well received, even if not perfectly understood at the time.

The things that were understood were these concepts: Without change we may die. Without change we stay a sub-culture. Without change others die without Christ. I wish I could say that these five or six sessions were all it took, but it did not even represent the foundation; they were basically the trenches into which the concrete would be poured. It was, however, a start.

God Intervenes

During this process, something happened to me that I can only describe as a "before and after" event.

In the 1998 movie, *Fallen*, Denzel Washington played Detective John Hobbs. Hobbs has become consumed by an investigation that had consumed the life of decorated policeman Robert Milano some twenty years earlier, ending in that officer's disgrace. While looking around an isolated cabin, the site of the previous officer's death, the Hobbs character does a voice over narration, saying, "There are moments which mark your life-moments when you realize that things will never be the same. And time is divided into two parts: before this and after this."

My moment met me in 2004.

I was standing at the rear door of our auditorium, greeting the Sunday morning's guests when a man walked over to me. He and I had met before, but I had not seen him in a long while. As I turned to speak, this man grasped my outstretched hand while putting his free hand around my head and pulling it close to his so that he could speak into my ear. He spoke to me in this manner for about two minutes. The following is a portion of his spoken words:

> "Marty, I'm here today because I believe that God has given me something to tell you. The only reason that I came this morning was to tell you

this. I've been praying for you and I think that God wants me to tell you this-do what He has put it into your heart to do. What you've been praying about is from Him and He will be with you if you do it.

"You need to be prepared to suffer the consequences and go through whatever might happen. You may lose your job, but you must be willing to do what God wants you to do. He's calling you to do this. He has put this in your heart. Do what He is telling you to do.

"I think that the Lord wanted me to tell you this."

I pulled my head back, somewhat stunned, and watched him and his wife walk away. There is no telling what else transpired that morning; I do not remember. I do not even remember if I thanked him for his words.

I fully understand the scriptural admonition to test spirits and fully understand the danger of speaking when God has not spoken. So as not to run off half-cocked, I called three pastor friends--one was the pastor with whom I has spent so much time pondering God's work in our locale, second the former pastor mentioned before whom I had befriended and, third, was Todd Wright. I told each of them in turn what had happened. "I know him, but I don't know any way that he could have known to tell me that. Before Sunday, I had not seen him in two years. What do you think about what happened?" Two of them said immediately, "I believe that this was God speaking to you and you need to pay attention." The third one said, "I cannot say for sure, but it certainly could be of God and if it is then it will come to pass."

That encounter was the last thing I expected. I'm not typically given to waiting for God to speak through others; I'm usually listening for Him to speak primarily through His Word. However, after counsel and prayer, I did receive it as God's encouragement to me that I might follow and trust Him regarding all He had put on my heart. I knew that my responsibility was to obey (John 2:5); the results were out of my hands.

Who am I?

As we began to move more intentionally into the transition, one of the first changes I instituted was removing the pulpit from the stage and replacing it with a stool. I did not do this because some other big name preacher was doing it, but I had seen it done and liked the atmosphere that it conveyed to the listeners. I know of some contemporary pastors who use a table or some style of podium and it works just fine for them. For me, there was a still bigger issue involved.

The man who had been my pastor during my most formative years of ministry was an old time fireball preacher. He beat against the pulpit, shouted and hollered-it was revival style preaching at its best. He was a wonderful expositor of the Word and under his preaching my wife and I grew amazingly. However, that kind of impact posed a problem for me after getting into ministry myself. Though I had listened to hundreds, if not thousands of hours of preaching on cassette tapes and in person (from pastors to evangelists to

Bible conference speakers), and though every imaginable style was represented in that listening, my preaching style was almost identical to that of my former pastor. In a way, he was preaching through me. People who had been members of my home church would tell me, "You preach *just like* Brother _____."

Now, if they had been referring merely to my exegetical skill, then that would have been an awesome and wonderful compliment. But they were not and I knew it. They were speaking of style. I would often have people ask me, "Why are you so mad when you preach?" when I was not upset. Even Sonya (my wife) would periodically say, "You really seemed upset this morning when you preached." But I was not. At least one person left our church after stating, "I just feel like I'm beaten down every week during the sermon." I realize that part of that sentiment was personal perception since there were other people who did not feel the same way, but it bothered me that some people had perceived an anger that did not exist.

It took a great while for me to recognize that I was not even being myself while I was preaching-I was being my former pastor. It was a shocking revelation. A further realization came as I understood that my preaching style was tied to the presence of the pulpit and that I continued to preach in a hard and berating style when I stood behind it.

So, I took it out and put a bar stool in its place. For me it had to be that drastic.

For three or four Sundays I actually sat down to deliver the message. I figured, "If Jesus can do it, why can't I?" (Matt. 5:1, 2) Ultimately, my natural tendency toward walking around took over and I only placed only my Bible, not myself, on the stool. It remains my primary prop while communicating today.

In addition to removing the pulpit, the issue of style was further addressed when I made a conscious attempt to become more conversational in tone, rather than fiery and loud. Again, it related to me attempting to be preaching with my own personality, rather than my former pastor's personality. If Phillips Brooks was right that, "Preaching is truth communicated through personality," then to be using another personality was an affront to the God who has made me as I am!

I can remember being in the middle of the Sunday message and feeling myself get wound up almost to the level of volcanic eruption to make a point, when I would intentionally ratchet myself back a notch. The passion did not leave, but the "angry eyes" and stern countenance did. The effect was immediate with many people sharing their preference for the new communication style. One of our approving senior adults remarked, "It's almost like a fireside chat." It was a compliment gratefully accepted as I understood the historical reference.

God does not look...

Another transition, as it regarded my preaching, was that of the way that I dressed. As with many young preachers raised in the South I had learned to dress as well as I could on my budget. If three-piece suits were in style, then I bought them. If the style changed to two-piece, then I wore that. Slacks and a blazer? I was there. And, as with many preachers, I loved a handsome tie. Although I detested actually wearing the things, feeling as though I was being choked, I loved hearing, "Man, that's a sharp tie!" Or, when I went through my Looney Toons character tie phase, I wanted people to laugh at the face of Marvin the Martian or Taz peeking over my top jacket button.

At a Bible conference in the 1980s, before I actually entered the pastorate, I clearly remember a presenter admonishing us to, "button that top button on your jacket! There is nothing worse than having your jacket tail flying around while you preach. And dress nice! I'm not saying that you have to shop with the Three Hebrew Children (Hart, Schaffner and Marx), but do your best to look nice." I took all of it unquestioningly to heart.

The issue of dressing up finally came to a head within me as I considered the people around us. Our community was and is laid back with a prominent resort lake nearby. We have a huge Harley-Davidson dealer near us and, as anyone knows, suits are not first priority on a "hog." Lastly, the dominant age groupings around our campus are not the generations that dress up if giving the option to dress down. With the remembrance of my mission church days added, I just could not bear hearing again, "I can't go to church there because I don't have good enough clothes." Saying: "It doesn't matter what you wear" only goes so far when a person can look around them on Sunday and see that it obviously does matter.

So, I lost the suits and started wearing black jeans, black shirts and black shoes. It did elicit the inevitable Johnny Cash comparisons, but it was important to me that my clothes not be a distraction from the truths that I wanted to convey each Sunday. I asked our band and choir to do the same for a while and most complied even if they were not fully convinced that it was necessary. The goal was that we focus on God and His Word during that one hour and fifteen minutes each Sunday and that we could better accomplish that goal by taking the focus off the people on the stage.

Whether those specific things had an immediate impact, I'm not sure, but the emphasis on dressing down has had a huge impact on how our members dress on Sunday mornings and how new people respond as a result. Lost people do not feel threatened by church people dressing to impress and, contrary to warnings by the occasional overly dramatic critic, no one has worn their pajamas to church. There also has not been a "casual attitude toward God" as I was also warned. What we hear regularly is that there is a feeling of warmth that people do not experience in other churches that they have attended.

The overall goal in the "stage" changes from adding the stool to preaching style to clothing was singular:

communication. Communication is not the *giving* of information, it is the *exchange* of information meaning that the hearer needs to process and understand the words, phrases and ideas before an exchange-true communication-has taken place. My history-heavy sermon illustrations gave way to props such as sand in jars, chainsaws, weed eaters, hams carved during the message, video clips, audio clips, energy drinks audience participation, basically anything to keep the attention of the ones I desired to teach using forms that more readily created the opportunity for them to process and retain the truth that I was trying desperately to teach.

These attempted changes were not without challenges. One Sunday our Creative Arts Team put together a skit based on the U2 song, *I Still Haven't Found What I'm Looking For.* Among the players in this drama was a young lady who had only been saved for a short time. She was asked to play the part of a rough acting kind of woman and she agreed. To look the part, she decided to wear one of her old outfits that had been pushed to the back of her closet. Imagine my shock to walk into the auditorium and see her dressed in a "hoochie momma" top and mini-skirt ready to go onstage!

God was gracious in me to demonstrate grace to her. Had I come across as judgmental and harsh she could have been spiritually damaged for a long time. As it was, the drama went as scheduled, we dodged a bullet and she now dresses as modestly as any lady I know.

Community

We knew going into this transition that the planned change from traditional Sunday School to small groups built around community, meeting in homes at times other than Sunday mornings was the potential back breaker. This had originally been scheduled for the third year of the transition, but during our staff planning retreat in January of 2005 we came to the conclusion that we needed to accelerate the last phase by an entire year, moving to home groups in August of that year rather than August of 2006. When that suggestion flew out into the air of the North Georgia cabin where we were staying, every pastor in the room knew what was at stake. We paused, took a deep breath and began discussing what it would entail to move in that direction at that speed.

The argument that carried the day was that we would actually lose the moment if we waited. We had already gained all there was to gain in preparation and further delay would be a negative and make an already challenging transition even more difficult.

The organizational style of home group ministry on which we were the most sold was the model espoused by Randy Frazee, then of Pantego Bible Church in Dallas, Texas, in his book *The Connecting Church*. We knew that it would present some challenges, but were convinced that the concept of community that he taught was much closer to a biblical representation of the Christian life than the hurried, meeting-centric church experience that most of us had come to know.

The central tenet of Frazee's paradigm is that home groups should be based primarily on geography, not age. In fact, multiple generations in a single home group should be desired and not avoided. This made the most sense to us as a strategy for moving out of the "mother ship" (the main campus) and getting into our communities. That is not even to take into consideration the millions of dollars saved over time in classroom space that does not need to be built. Home groups had the potential to have the presence of an Acts 2 community in almost every subdivision where we had a member. Was not this what it was all about? We thought so and planned in that direction.

Returning from staff retreat, we immediately formed small groups to begin casting the vision. Each pastor would meet with five or six leaders to study through *The Connecting Church* with the goal of informing and preparing our people for this transition as well as answering the inevitable questions that would arise. This proved to be successful, though if we had it to do over again, we would have included about twice as many leaders in these discipleship groups as we did. As it was, we were farther along the road of preparation than we had ever been.

The Big Step

In August of 2005, we moved all adult Sunday School classes off campus. Since we simultaneously discontinued our Sunday evening services, most groups chose to meet on Sunday nights. The only groups that remained as Sunday

School classes were our senior adult classes and one class provided for anyone whose schedule would not allow them to participate in a home group.

It should be noted that in our research and study into home groups, we had spoken with the pastor of small groups at another church about our planned transition. His counsel, which we did not follow, was to make an announcement on one Sunday that we were doing away with Sunday School and starting home groups the next week! As if it was not hard enough to accomplish, we did not need that debacle to work through.

In addition, we expanded our children's worship (which we call Compass Kids) to include up to 5th grade (from 2nd grade) and started a youth worship service. Essentially, each age group met together so that they might hear teaching at their own level. In our strategy, home groups would be the place where parents and children could learn together. The goal was to create an environment where children could hear their parents praying and talking about the things of God, hopefully a situation that would make its way into their individual homes on a regular basis. In the traditional model, people are grouped by ages and grades during the time that discussion takes place (Sunday School) and are grouped together when no discussion takes place (the worship service). The result is that there is little, if any, cross-generational learning. Our pastors felt that this should be productively addressed, and home groups provided the format for that to happen.

It was my view that much of the traditional structure of church, rather than encouraging parent-child discipleship, actually hindered it. In the traditional structure, all activities take place with each generation separated from the others. We have nursery, children's church, "big" church and then, in larger churches, further breakdowns with middle and high school, college ministry, young adult, young married, median adult, etc. From the cradle to the grave in church structure we are segregated by age. For six consecutive years (middle and high school), most church kids are dropped off at the door for some activity and picked up three hours later. All discipleship is expected to be performed by the student pastor, while few if any spiritual conversations take place between parents and children in the home or anywhere else. And, God forbid, when little Sally or little Junior get caught with drugs or when Mom and Dad found out that their kid had been sneaking around having sex, then the Student Pastor, or the church, is at fault. It was our view that to continue in a structure that inhibited home based discipleship rather than encouraged and facilitated it was to be in sin as leaders. This is what we wanted to begin to change and we felt as if community through home groups was the most biblical model to propel those ideas.

And so it was that from January 2005 until August 2005 we planned in earnest for the transition to Home Groups. Several months out, we placed signs all over the facility that ready, "The Journey Begins...August 14." Taking Rick Warren's counsel to heart-"When you are sick of hearing it, they've just heard it once"-we tried to emphasize and explain as best we could.

One of the last pivotal messages that I preached used an illustration of Moses standing at the banks for the Red Sea with an antsy people waiting and an angry Pharaoh with full army closing in the rear view mirror (Ex. 14). Although Moses knew that God was going to do something (vs. 13, 14) he initially didn't know what was going to happen. My point to our congregation was that we were standing on the banks of our Red Sea and I could not say for sure *exactly* what was going to happen, but I believed that if we would trust God, then He would act in a mighty way to bring glory to Himself by demonstrating His strength through us. On Sunday, August 14, 2005, we launched out on what would soon become the ride of my pastoral ministry.

Implementation and Reaction
Chapter 5, part 1 (Todd)

No Risk! No Reward!

Up until I fully surrendered my life to Christ at the age of nineteen, I had never been much of a risk-taker. Until then, perhaps the biggest risk I had ever taken was to tell a beautiful blonde 6th grade girl I was going to marry her. I was a ripe old 8th grader myself. It backfired in my face. "Leave me alone, you greasy-headed fat slob!" was her response. It was a long journey, but several years later, I did marry that girl. Our wonderful marriage of more than twenty-five years continues to remind me that the greatest things life has to offer usually require great risk, but they are worth it. They require risk, time and hard work. Without risk, it's impossible to reach our greatest potential. The very nature of risk says that failure and disaster could follow the risk just as easily as success. But how would a person ever know unless they tried?

I was very much aware of the risks attached to this new journey of transitioning our church, but there was one key component that helped me move forward more than any other. It was the real sense that God was and is leading me down this path. For me, not to follow through would be blatant disobedience to the God who made me and called me to serve and lead in His kingdom. Personally, life was much more calm and peaceful when I was blind to the real disconnect and ineffectiveness that existed between the church and the unchurched. Since we had the fastest growing church in our area, I could go to bed every night feeling like a great success. I was completely unaware that the unchurched population in our area was growing with each passing year, but for me personally, life was great. I was becoming an expert! Leaders of other churches sometimes called to ask me about our growth. They would look for key principles and strategies that might work for them.

The fact was that I did know how to draw a crowd of Christians, but could I lead a movement of people to reach the thousands of unchurched in our region? Many of the things I felt God wanted me to do were things I had preached against. I would be required to undo so much of what I had implemented in the past. Nobody in their right mind would choose to enter such a journey on their own. It had taken an act of God to awaken me and lead me down this path! Now, however, God had chosen to use me to help awaken the church and lead them!

The Process Toward Change

The 10/10 Vision Summit was officially over, but I could clearly see that the hard work was just beginning. By this time in our journey, we were already trying out some newer music. By most in the worship world, the music in our new services would have been described as "blended." Prior to this, it would have been described as "Southern gospel" and "gospel" songs from the hymn book. Now, it included most of the mainstream types and styles of music. However, many in our own fellowship were struggling. For the most part, the young people were thrilled to have a little music that connected with their culture, but they wanted more. Others felt with every new contemporary song, we were forsaking the faith. I received letters, signed and unsigned, from people who were frustrated. They wanted everything "the way it used to be." Between those two points of pressure, I usually felt like the bologna pressed tightly between two pieces of bread, about to be eaten. It was difficult for me to understand why and how three or four songs on the weekend could be such a big deal. Personally, I had a great appreciation for all types of music, from bluegrass to Beethoven. I loved to sing. In my lifetime, I had played the saxophone, piano, tuba and banjo. Besides, I could listen to "my kind of music" in the car as I traveled to and from church.

I had pulled together a vision steering team, made up from what we call our executive officers. Besides me, it included the chairpersons from three groups: our deacon ministry team, finance ministry team, and trustees. My executive pastor also served to help me communicate and implement the details of every decision to all of our staff and volunteers. Their leadership and support would be imperative if we were going to move forward successfully.

Our vision steering team agreed that we should attempt to address the music problem at the same time we presented the ten new initiatives. Our solution was to change our 9:15 a.m. Sunday service back to Southern gospel, hymns, and gospel songs from the hymnal. Our 10:45 a.m. Sunday service would be more contemporary in style, but would still include our choir. One of the new initiatives was a Saturday night service. It was there we hoped to connect with the younger generation in an intentional way. We openly referred to it as music and worship on steroids.

We knew that we couldn't continue to add new initiatives without taking away some of our previous programming. Since we were creating a Saturday night service, we decided we would no longer have a Sunday night service. Our Sunday nights were fun for some, but for staff and preschool workers, it made for a long tiring day. It was made up of a remnant of committed churchgoers who had been present on Sunday morning. They had worshipped and heard a great message (hopefully) on Sunday morning and would come back to church on Sunday night for another message. There was little time in between to reflect on and apply truth from the Sunday morning service before more truth was piled on top of it.

Figuratively, all of us were still rubbing our eyes from our long spiritual naps, but regardless, it was time to go to work. With the vision steering team by my side on the platform on Sunday, September 25, 2005, I carefully introduced these new concepts to our church, along with all of the ten new initiatives. I explained that we would be giving immediate attention to redesigning our Sunday services and focusing on a Saturday night service. This strategy would create a "win" seemingly for every group in the church. We would also focus on home teams in addition to Sunday School, community partnerships, and improve our internal communication systems and processes. In the months and years ahead, we would work on the other initiatives. I explained that God had blessed us in many ways, but the best was yet to come.

On that Sunday evening, we had a question and answer time about everything I had presented on Sunday morning. The people seemed to be somewhat OK with everything except canceling Sunday night services. Even some people who seldom came on Sunday night were against it! I had to explain that neither our staff nor I would last at our current pace. If we were going to do things with excellence, we would have to do fewer things!

Damage Control

Overall everything seemed to be going as planned, but beneath the surface, all was not well. One key team member had their own agenda and began to sow seeds of fear and skepticism to some about our new direction. When I confronted this person about the destructive nature of their actions, they didn't change their attitude or actions, but simply became more careful. This person also refused to work with another key team member in our future journey. They decided to leave the church and sent a misleading and damaging email to many in the church. If they had wanted to create confusion and dissension in our church family, they were definitely successful. Alliances were built. There had been a refusal to be a part of the team, and now there was an obvious intent to bring about difficulty on their way out. That person left Midway suddenly and went to serve in another church in the community. Several other families followed them to their new place of service in the weeks ahead. In the midst of all the confusion, others simply left and went to different established churches in the community that had good Southern gospel music. Still others went to be a part of a church we had intentionally planted only a few weeks earlier in a neighboring county. There were many others at Midway who were confused as to what had happened and why.

A spirit of distrust toward me and our new direction had been planted and was spreading like wildfire. At best, it was a mess, and somebody had to clean it up. At the time, there was a part of me that would have preferred to get a one-way ticket to Timbuktu.

However, I had learned a long time ago that it is the responsibility of every leader to cast vision, build teams, remove obstacles and clean up messes.

It was the first sign of failure on a journey that had been started with good intentions. I thought to myself, "So much for all of my teaching about teamwork!" I admit I immediately wondered if I should continue to lead Midway through this transition or go and establish a new church altogether, but I wanted to believe that old historic churches could transition and become vibrant movements of God once again.

My staff leadership team and I met with our deacons, executive officers and a couple of choir leaders we felt could help bring stability to the situation. Our meeting had a sense of urgency to it since the person who left gave me only two days notice before Sunday. There were major responsibilities for the weekend that were left undone. In our meeting we attempted to discuss and gain wisdom about the best ways to move forward in light of the current dissension. We wanted to make sure the church functioned as smoothly as possible in the weeks ahead.

There was obvious confusion and distrust in my own inner circle as a result of things that had been said or sent through e-mail from this individual. For some, it appeared that my integrity had been brought into question as a result. An undeserved dark cloud of resentment and distrust was also placed over another outstanding staff member who was mentioned in the e-mail. It was like spilled milk that couldn't be put back in the cup. A negative perception of me had been sown into the minds of some of my key leaders and closest friends, and I couldn't make it suddenly disappear.

As I began our meeting, in an attitude of honesty and humility I explained exactly what had happened. I explained it was up to each individual whether or not to believe me. All of them were outstanding people who had faithfully served alongside me for many years. I knew some of them had been told things I could not erase from their minds with one meeting. I even asked them, once again, to carefully consider whether or not they wanted to go down this new journey with me. "If you don't believe I am the person to lead Midway from this point on, please give me a few months to discern where God wants me to be," I stated. "My time at Midway has been the most fulfilling time of my life. I have led you with integrity since 1996. I am attempting to do so through this journey also. I cannot deny this new stirring from God in my heart about the next generation and the unchurched.

"Before it's over there will probably be many more who will leave Midway as a result of our new direction," I confessed. "It's just the nature of change. I know it will be difficult, but I'm committed to the journey. If you don't want to go this route, I fully understand. There are no hard feelings. It just means our time together at Midway will be over." Once again I received their commitment to continue with me on our journey together and we agreed to do everything possible to keep our church moving forward. They wanted me to continue as the leader of Midway. We didn't know what the future held, but we agreed to experience it together.

We made it through that first weekend after the key leader had left, but to be perfectly honest, emotionally I was a wounded basket case. There was a part of me that wondered if God was anywhere to be found. There were many concerns to deal with as a result of this conflict. I knew there had been times when people had lost their lives or had been sent to prison while obediently following Christ. Was He leading me down a path that would end in failure and total humiliation? I had to come to grips with that possibility if it was in the plan of God. Did I really hear from God regarding this new direction? Had God been satisfied with our church the way it was before we started our transition? Were some people correct to say I had only "messed up a good thing"? It had been suggested that I was perhaps going through a midlife crisis. Speaking about me, someone commented, "Any day now, he might drive up in a new convertible sports car, wearing some gold chains around his neck!"

I realized we had the potential to lose several more families. We had just started construction on some new facilities to expand our small group ministry to preschoolers, children and students. The project had an estimated cost of almost nine million dollars. Our new bank payment would be almost seventy thousand dollars per month. I didn't know it at the time, but including those we sent to plant an additional new church and the others who left in the conflict, approximately two hundred regular attendees would leave within a three month period. Our offerings would drop $7,000-$10,000 per week for several weeks. Some who remained in the church also held back their tithes and offerings, hoping that the financial pressure would force us to "take it back to the way things used to be."

A Word from God

After that first weekend, I received a phone call while I was at the gym one morning. So much was going on inside of me, my outward appearance probably resembled a zombie more than a victorious Christian. The day before, I had prayed, "God I've been doing all of the talking, but I've got to hear from You. If I don't hear from You, I don't know how much longer I can continue! I need an affirmation that I'm still on the right track." I felt numb inside and out. I questioned everything that had transpired throughout the weekend. I wondered what the future held.

The phone call I received was from a local businessman and a committed Christian. He was a part of another church in the area. At the time, I had not spoken to him or seen him in several months, maybe a year. With quivering voice, he carefully chose his words and asked if he could meet with me that morning. He said it was urgent. I agreed to go by his office upon leaving the gym. When I arrived, he was sitting behind his desk with tears in his eyes. He explained that during his prayer time that morning, God spoke to him about me. He said, "I don't know what you think about such things, but I saw images of Midway and you. God spoke to my heart about where you are in your journey with Him. I wrote what I saw as best as I could. And God wanted me to share this with you today."

He then gave me a handwritten, three-page letter that I will keep as a lifelong treasure. It began "The Word of the Lord to Pastor Todd." Wow! That was a little heavy. To some, it would appear to be super spiritual arrogance and presumptuousness. Others would perhaps consider it to be spiritual giftedness gone wild. However, his teary eyes and humble broken spirit told me that he had been with God that morning. The letter seemed to be broken into three segments. First, there was an affirmation of God's call upon my life. Second was mention of a "rebellious Jezebel spirit" revealing itself through a couple of leaders in our church, with others blindly following. God would deal with them in His own way and give me wisdom to clean up the mess. Many would leave, but some would return. Third, there was a description of the future in our journey as a church:

> "God has given you a new machine to glean the fields with. It is new, different, a change, much more advanced. It is more efficient. It will get rid of the chaff, trash and weeds. It will be a process on how to use it and all its workings. Once you get it all going it will glean and clean. The harvest is very ripe. You are one of the many combines in the mighty and ripe field. God trusted you with a good machine. Now He is getting you ready, to get you into a mightier, more efficient and productive machine.
>
> "And this is the word of the Lord that is given to you this day."

Though some might be skeptical, there was no doubt to me that God had spoken. For the next couple of days I withdrew to pray and fellowship with God. I wept often, but they were tears of renewal and awe. I was in the midst of a storm, but I had joy and confidence beyond measure. Yes. The journey ahead would be a challenge, but I would walk it with God's hand upon me.

Turning the Dream into Ministry

Over the next few weeks and months, we put teams together to help implement each new initiative that I had presented. I tried to show love to the people, regardless of how they felt about the changes. I refused to speak negatively about those who had left. We tightened our budget and attempted to raise addition income through some special offerings. We connected with the truly unchurched through community events such as Trunk-a-Treat, special Christmas Eve services and a large Easter Egg hunt. We started our Saturday night service and tailored Sunday mornings to two different groups. We began Crosspoint, an outreach worship service at the campus of The State University of West Georgia. We developed a new simple way to communicate our vision and strategy, calling it "The Five Star Focused Church." The five components were: 1. Love God, 2. Love People, 3. Serve the World, 4. Invite Others, 5. Give Generously. We converted our Sunday School to L.I.F.E. groups that can meet anywhere, anytime of the week in addition to meeting on campus each Sunday. Their purpose would be to Love People, Investigate God's Word, Fellowship Together, and Evangelize Unbelievers. One year later, when we finished our church year in August, we had grown by fourteen percent in our small group ministry. We had lost almost two hundred regular attendees, but still had a net growth of fourteen percent. That was double the growth rate from the year before.

We began using our additional new facilities in September 2006. We had a grand opening and dedication ceremony, with a festival for the children and free hot dogs for the community. Thousands came. In the weeks ahead, we saw new faces every weekend. One entire family gave their lives to Christ only one week after attending the fair. Again, we had our Trunk-a-Treat outreach for Halloween, and we added a drive-through, live nativity, with live camels, for Christmas. Thousands came over three days. One of our deacons led regular outreach block parties at two different apartment sites. We had weekly ministry in the local jails. We had English classes for Latinos in the area. We had weekly ministry in a nearby Senior Adult Care center. The people in the church were personally involved in getting people to the church, and in taking the church to the people.

Adjustments on the Journey

There were great signs of life, but soon, some more difficult adjustments would be required. Our 9:15 a.m. Sunday worship service was not connecting or growing. During the conflict in the fall of 2005, many of our Southern gospel-type musicians had left. We consistently used those who remained for solos and quartets, but it never seemed to be enough. For some, they were simply missing some of the musicians who had left, and there was nothing we could do to replace them. Almost every week, somebody from that service complained about the music, even though to the best of our ability it was being tailored to them and their culture. That particular service had originally begun with about 325 people, but had shrunk to less than two hundred. Our 10:45 a.m. service, more contemporary in style, had begun with about six hundred people and had grown to over eight hundred in our thousand-seat worship center. I brought in two different consultants to help us see things clearly. Both stated that unless this imbalance was addressed, our growth would again come to a halt soon.

Once again I met with our staff, executive officers, and deacons to discuss this issue. We concluded that rather than starting an additional Sunday service or build a new worship facility, we should make both Sunday services exactly alike. They would be much like the current 10:45 a.m. service, with some rendition of a hymn often incorporated into the mix. We could then keep both services balanced by asking people to shift from one service to another. It was now January 2007, and we felt like the best time to make this adjustment would be on Easter Sunday, when things were a little chaotic anyway. In anticipation, we planned a special church-wide Sunday night gathering in February so we could communicate this information and attempt to gain the church's full support.

The numbers and facts were clear, and the best solution was obvious to all. It was not a win for everyone, but it was a win for the mission of the church. We made that adjustment and continued to grow. In many ways we were making great progress, but some were ultimately disappointed with making both of our Sunday worship services identical. Some felt betrayed. As a result, several more established families left in the following months.

Signs of Progress

At the time of this writing it is December 2007. We closed out another church year in August with news that our L.I.F.E. Group ministry grew by twenty-two percent. We have more people than ever, but offerings continue to be a challenge. They, too, are slowly growing again, but our vision seems to consistently grow at a faster rate than our income. Some people who don't like our new direction still hold back their offerings from Midway, even though they have chosen to stay and take advantage of our exciting and growing church. Wise stewardship, family financial training and good financial management is a major priority for us during these days. However, God has been faithful. We baptized more new believers last year than any other year in our 160-year history, and since the new church year began in September, five to fifteen people per month follow Christ in believer's baptism and the average age of attendees is thirty-seven.

Our journey continues to be risky, but every week, I see people of all races at Midway: red, yellow, black and white, worshipping and serving in God's kingdom together. I see several older people attempting to understand and minister to the next generation. I see young people who passionately love and serve God with great dependability. I see established, middle-aged adults who invest financially into reaching the next generation. My thoughts about my vision have evolved from "What if..." to "Maybe so!" There is beginning to be light at the end of the tunnel. We will continue to evaluate and strive for excellence in all five components of our Five Star Focus.

When I came to Midway in 1996, it seemed like I climbed into a single engine Cessna, but throughout our journey it had evolved into a 747 jetliner. We were flying higher than ever and there were more people on the journey than we had originally dreamed. However, now we hoped to evolve into a massive space shuttle, prepared to take thousands to a place called heaven, far beyond the starry skies.

Chapter 5, part 2 (Marty)

"Besides the other things, what comes upon me daily: my deep concern for all the churches."

The Apostle Paul

First Things Second

My first pastorate began in 1989 at the previously mentioned church-a country church south of Atlanta. I was as green as a pastor could be: I was twenty-five years old when called, with no seminary training or pastoral experience in any role. The sum total of my "leadership experience" was Vacation Bible School, Sunday School and Discipleship Training. I was woefully unprepared.

So, I did what I knew to do which was preach hard and try to win people to Christ. God blessed us to see a number of people saved and baptized; the first year was a dream. Then, as is so often the case, the honeymoon ended and I began to run afoul of the established leadership in the church. Without doubt I made errors in leading and the "authoritarian" model of pastor-deacon relations I emulated certainly brought with it unnecessary conflict.

After a very rough stretch during which I was under a lot of stress, there was a point when my treasurer gave me a "heads up" that the deacons were going to question me about the phone bill being too high. I remember a Sunday morning when, as a twenty-seven-year-old pastor, I was fearful to exit my study thinking that I was going to be roped into a secret meeting just before service time. A knock on my door went unanswered as tearfully I phoned a friend down the road and asked him to pray for me that I could make it through the morning. He did and I did.

I have a distinct memory of my chairman of deacons coming over to the pastorium and questioning me, then threatening me with dismissal over my desire to lead the church to reach the community, no matter who the community might be. He said, "Marty, everywhere we go now we have to be around blacks. Church is about the only place where people feel like they can get away from them." When I did not adopt his point of view, he informed me, "You are on your way out!"

I asked, "On whose authority, yours?"

"On the church's authority," He responded.

"Well," I said, "if the church decides for me to leave, then I'll go. But, I'm not leaving just because you want me to leave." It was more than a little tense.

A few months later, I stood to read my letter of resignation and shortly left the church; the entirety of my tenure being just over two years. The pain of that "failed" pastorate could not possibly be surpassed, I did not think.

I was wrong.

A Greater Pain

I knew that transitioning a church was going to be difficult and I had tried to prepare the body for what was to come. A dilemma that I faced early was whether to put the planned transition to a vote of the church. It would have been the easiest way out, but I was pretty sure of the outcome-it would fail. Our entire pastoral staff was convinced of the direction that God wanted us to go and all of us were "in for a penny; in for a pound," having already decided that if the church refused to transition that we would resign en masse and start a new church based on what we believed God was leading us to do.

We did not vote. Looking back, I know this was the right decision, but it was not any easy one. The church had duly called me to pastor and I believed-as shepherd-that I was to lead the sheep to green pastures even if the sheep were completely content in the field where they were. I knew that things were going to be difficult enough as it was without a permanent record of how divided the flock might have been.

Alerting the body about what was coming became a top priority with me. By this time, virtually all of the actual troublesome members had already left so the issue was going to be with good people who simply could not, or would not, catch the vision. Speaking in groups and individually, I and our other pastors tried to prepare the church for the coming exodus. It had actually already started but, I knew, was to intensify for a period of time. What I really needed was someone to prepare *me*.

I watched as individuals and families left, never to return. Many ended up at the same church up the road from us-a church which had a much more traditional structure of music, preaching and ministry. In fact, it appeared that those folks were essentially looking to replace in their "church life" what they had lost during our transition. A few others went to another church in our area only to face the same issues when that church went into a transition similar to ours! I must confess that I chuckled when I found out about that.

There was the man who left because he felt pressured by someone to serve in an area of ministry. And then there was the woman who said, "We're leaving, but we're not telling Marty. He'll find out when the tithe check stops coming." I guess she was not aware that I do not check members' giving records. Then there were those that never gave a reason.

Our pastoral staff understood that we could not chase these folks down trying to convince them to stay. Virtually all of them were leaving after months of trying to determine whether they still fit at New Bethany. This was even more difficult because a shepherd's natural tendency is to protect his sheep; in this instance, we had to be willing for them to entrust themselves to the leadership of another shepherd while we looked for sheep that were "not of this fold."

I repeated over and over, "These are not bad people. They are just people who cannot see where it is we believe God wants us to go." It was difficult, especially when I suspected the deeper reason for some was as simple as not wanting the kind of journey that I was proposing. It frustrated all of our pastors that some people actually *preferred* a static, rather than dynamic, relationship with God. We remained committed to staying with the transition, even as it began to cost us in more ways than attendance.

Financial Problems

Following the terror attacks of September 11, 2001, our offerings dropped, a reality faced by many churches. But now our offerings began to drop to a disturbing level. Our pastors faced the real possibility of losing our incomes or at the very least becoming bivocational until we made it through the drop in giving. We were running far behind our basic weekly requirements; a few people questioned how we were even making it week to week. If there was anyone who measured success strictly by monies received, then we were a dismal failure.

One thing that I started understanding only after it took effect was that people who were saved with no real prior biblical background did not immediately start tithing. In fact, from counsel I received with other pastors in the same situation, I learned that two years was not an unusual time frame before the "conversion of the pocketbook" (as Martin Luther termed it) took place. Our pastors made the decision, in the fall of 2006 that we would all go part-time in January 2007. We did not see any way that the level of tithes and offerings being given would sustain both full-time salaries and fully implemented ministries. (In another story for another time, God made it possible for that step to not be necessary, but it was a reality we faced. It was with extraordinary faith that all of our pastors—Dan Brothers, Ronnie Cansler, Joey Jernigan and Brandan Lail—never wavered at this nor sent out resumes to get out of it. I'm incredibly honored to serve with them.)

One of the most difficult things for me to deal with personally was that, though we had entered the transition with the purpose of being more effective at reaching the unchurched and de-churched in our community, our rate of baptisms continued to fall. Each and every year was lower than the one previous with the exception of two consecutive years of the same number. On more than one occasion went long periods of time without seeing a person come to faith in Christ, and some that did would not follow in baptism. This weighed heavier on me than virtually anything. Frankly, I could not understand why God would not send His Spirit in power, if for no other reason than to validate what He had led us to do. My ultimate conclusion was that because of the uncertainty in our congregation, not much evangelization was taking place. My hope was that once we were through the transition we would begin to see the harvest for which we had longed.

As the hemorrhage of membership continued, our strongest lay leaders sometimes struggled with how much farther it might go. "We've just lost so many good people" was a common sentiment expressed to me. I knew it as well, because it was true. That began within me a true crisis of my leadership and for the first time I really wondered if indeed I would make it as the lead pastor.

Crushed

That crisis was intensified at a Monday evening meeting with my pastoral leadership team, a group of five men who advise me, counsel me and help me be a better leader. They have freedom to ask me anything and I have the freedom to request anything of them. On this particular evening, I began to express to them my frustration about people who would not follow God and were thus compounding the difficulties in the church.

Immediately, one of the men said, "I don't agree with that. Why is it that every time that something goes wrong in the church that it is the people's fault? Why isn't it ever the pastor's fault?" Those questions opened the way for what was, for me at least, a most unpleasant evening.

I listened as most of them shared the mistakes that they believed me to be making. I was charged with being unapproachable, woefully lacking in clear communication, not listening well, of appearing uncaring and a few other not very flattering descriptions. After about ninety minutes of things I was doing wrong, the meeting ended with a single affirmation: I was "an amazing preacher."

Though I managed to maintain my composure externally, inside I was very hurt and very angry. I felt ambushed and alone and that as a leader and pastor I was pretty much of a failure and that if I could not even win over my leadership team, there was not much hope for winning the rest of the body. As best as I could, I received all of this correction and tried to determine if anything could be done about it or whether I was finished at New Bethany. One of the group called me later to make sure that I was okay and, as I remember, I lied and said that I was.

Though more frustrated than at any time since, I recognized that these men had said what they said with good intent and proper motives. These were men who had given their allegiance to me as the lead pastor and I knew they loved me and were concerned about my ministry. It eventually hit me that if those that cared the most for my successful ministry had seen all these weaknesses, how much more confused and frustrated were those who were still on the fence about the entire transition. I quickly realized that I had a decision: act or react. If I reacted, then I would loose credibility and it would be recognized that I could not take constructive criticism from the very ones I had invited into my life for that very role. If I took what they said to heart and acted in a way to correct the problems, then my ministry influence could probably and would probably be restored.

After a lot of self-searching, I remained convinced that some people had left for the reasons listed above. But, I had to confess that my leadership flaws had worsened the situation to a level that it need not have gone. Actually this should not have caught me completely by surprise. One of the most intense discussions surrounding our home group transition was with my wife as I attempted to articulate what I thought we needed to do and why. The more questions she asked, the more frustrated I became. I felt as if she was not supportive and she felt I'd lost my mind. I should have seen it as a harbinger of larger scale communication problems.

A Good Decision

By the next pastoral staff meeting, I had decided what I would do. We would have congregational prayer meetings on every Sunday night for the next month (July 2006). Anyone who wanted to attend could come. We all sat on the floor at the front of the auditorium and prayed for three or four Sunday nights. On the last Sunday morning of the July, I announced that I would be addressing the congregation that night and encouraged everyone to attend and many did.

As I reflected on all the feedback I had received, I realized my reactions had exacerbated the problems that we faced. Without meaning to do so, I had begun anticipating bad news and negative comments, responding in advance by withdrawing from interaction. This was not intentional, but during those darkest months I found it impossible to both survive and thrive, so pulling back was the most natural solution. Maybe it was a defense mechanism, but it led to very poor communication on my part. I anticipated bad news, so I avoided talking with people. This led to more walls being built, which perpetuated the cycle.

My talk to the church was to publicly and without excuse take the blame for all the shortcomings that had happened in the two years of the transition and to ask forgiveness for those offenses. I asked anyone for whom a public repentance was insufficient to please see me privately. I asked the body to be patient as all of our pastors grew in our ability to communicate better. Then, I reminded our body that, since I had been their lead pastor for eight years (at that time) I was a known commodity—both my strengths and weaknesses were in the open. I further encouraged folks not to expect perfection from me and to be willing to speak with me on those occasions of failure.

The service was a watershed moment for us all. Owing to God's grace and an obedient and loving people, we rounded a corner. Some people who had struggled were reinvigorated spiritually and really bought into the vision that God had given to us those years before. In my view, that month and that Sunday night service were turning points for us. I sincerely and deeply hoped it was so.

A New Beginning
Chapter 6, Part 1 (Todd)

New!

I have always loved new beginnings! Just the word NEW makes my heart beat a little faster than normal—a new friend, a new bicycle, a new car, a new house, a new opportunity, a new restaurant, a new day, or a new year. It's a concept that God created, and obviously He loves to be a part of making things new. Anything or anyone that God really gets involved with becomes new. Too often, the local church is focused on keeping things old. They either ignore, or are blind to the fact that "old" is the last stage before death. All of the statistics about dying and plateaued churches today show that most are succeeding in their quest to preserve the old. Old things die! New things are vibrant with life!

The Bible speaks of a new creation, a new song, a new commandment, a new movement of the Spirit, a new covenant, a new life, a new heaven and a new earth. When a person comes to know Christ, that person becomes a "new creation, old things are passed away...all things become new."

Someday, when all of God's children gather together in a new heaven and a new earth, we will sing a new song. It's obvious to me that God loves "new." That's what spiritual re-new-al is all about.

As I look back, that's also what my journey over these last few years has been about. God is doing something new in my own life and in the church that He has called me to lead. I have learned that nothing becomes new automatically. There is a process that is involved. The very nature of "new" requires change. The very nature of change, from the human perspective, requires risk. The very nature of risk includes the potential for failure and pain, but it also includes the potential for something new, exciting and awesome.

It's actually a little too early in our journey to clearly declare any long-term victory, but the trends have certainly moved in favor of potential success and a bright future. I've already mentioned some of the specifics in chapter 5, but in order to communicate clearly, I will probably mention a few of them again, and even expand upon some of them. The results are multifaceted.

A New Pastor

First of all, the biggest changes and improvements have happened inside of me. I have openly shared with our church leadership and church family that I am a different pastor than the one who came to Midway in 1996. Through each phase of our journey thus far, the church has been remarkably patient, flexible and attentive to what God has done in the heart of their leader. It hasn't been easy for them or me, but our church has a much brighter future as a result of our willingness to change and move through the journey together. I have experienced God in this journey in a way that could never be learned from a book or group study. My understanding of, and appreciation for the church is greater than ever. I have a "kingdom" philosophy of ministry and a missional approach to life that is more exciting with each passing day.

By that, I mean every day is a fresh new opportunity to experience and express life with the God of all creation. I want every encounter in life to be an opportunity to represent God well, especially to the masses of humanity who don't know Jesus Christ.

I have a wholesome and healthy respect for all people in the body of Christ, both inside *and* outside of my own denominational background. While I understand that each local church must teach and adhere to its own biblical understanding and theological distinctiveness, I also look for ways to bring the body of Christ together for causes of world evangelism and leadership training.

However, there have been many times throughout the transition of the last four years that I have sunk to emotional lows. I've had to disappear from the crowds a few times to be restored mentally, emotionally and spiritually. At times, Sunday seemed to come too quickly every seven days, and nobody wants to listen to a discouraged and depressed pastor. At some points in the journey Sunday seemed little more than a time to be forced out of hiding and into the open fire of constant criticism and complaints each week before I got up to preach. "EVERYBODY thinks the music is too loud!" "NOBODY likes the new music!" "EVERYBODY is leaving the church!" "We want things to be the way they used to be!" My dear mother was even cornered in the ladies restroom at the church with a heartfelt plea, "Please ask Todd to start wearing ties again!"

During this phase of the journey, I learned what really refreshes me. It was a great thing to learn and something I continue to carry with me. Sometimes it's a simple honest prayer or a word from God. On other days it is special times with my wife, Lisa, or time with our two wonderful daughters, Hannah and Olivia. Their presence reminds me that, in reality, no success or person is more important to me in this life than they are. My journey with God demands that I must effectively love and lead them. Otherwise, I will not be able to effectively love and lead the church. To hang out with them and a couple of our best friends is sometimes all I need to be refreshed and to gain perspective. At other times, the greatest medicine has been to jump on my beautiful palomino horse and go for a ride. At one point, I even went out west with a true friend and mentor, to work as a cowboy on a cattle ranch. It was a great change of pace and scenery. Sometimes I love to play a round of golf with a friend who isn't going to complain or ask me a lot of church questions. At other times, I have to get on a plane and travel to some remote area of the world to invest time and leadership training with other pastors. I have to be reminded that the kingdom of God isn't locked inside the four walls of the church I lead, the denomination I belong to, nor the country or the culture I live in!

Through each phase of my journey, I seem to gain a better perspective regarding the real priorities of life. I have a greater understanding of who I am in Christ, who He wants me to be, and what He wants me to do. I have a better understanding of my own spiritual giftedness and unique callings. I am more confident and comfortable in my own skin than I have ever been in my life. I have a deeper appreciation for personal friends and other people on the team. Their uniqueness of gifts and their own calling before God are so much more important in my own spiritual journey than I ever dreamed. I am much more grateful for our differences. I can clearly see that it's our differences that make us better as a team. More than ever, I greatly treasure each team member. At this moment, I am a much better risk-taker for kingdom causes. Above all else, I want my life to count for the kingdom of God!

I am also beginning to understand more about real leadership during times of difficulty and crisis. Napoleon said, "Leaders are dealers in hope." I now know what he meant. When everything hurts, leaders must keep smiling, loving and leading. When everyone else has lost all hope, leaders must say, "Together, we can do it!" Nobody wants to follow a leader who isn't going anywhere; and nobody wants to follow a leader who is always in despair or one who doesn't believe in the future. The leader must be honest and transparent while at the same time providing hope and direction for the future. There has to be a high level of trust in the leader in order to follow him or her. "What people want in a leader is someone who is trustworthy, competent, has a vision of the future, and is dynamic and inspiring."[1] In short, they want a leader who is "real!"

I have also learned through this journey that I do not have to be the lead pastor of Midway to be who God wants me to be. My self-esteem, identity and worth is not summed up by one particular success or failure in one particular local church; rather it is summed up by a life lived on mission with Jesus Christ. It's about a lifetime of living, loving and leading to honor Him.

Many of these lessons are things I've been familiar with for years. I knew many of them theoretically and some of them were already a part of my character. But there are some things that can only be developed experientially through pain and hardship, followed by a right response. It was Job who said, "When He has tested me, I shall come forth as gold" (Job 23:10). In many ways, I feel like I did when God first called me and anointed me to preach and lead in His kingdom. There are people to be reached for the kingdom of God, and God has chosen me to be a part of His plan to reach them. *He* alone is my motivation, pursuit and audience—everything and everyone else is secondary! I feel like there is a new and adventurous life just around the corner, and I can hardly wait

---

[1] James M. Kouzes and Barry Z. Posner, *Credibility* (Jossey-Bass: San Francisco), 46.

to see what God will do in my life next!

A New Church

Secondly, there have been many changes in the life of the church that I lead. Midway has a new atmosphere. There is a sense of being a part of something fun and important all at the same time. Many would think that the word "fun" and "church" should not be in the same sentence. To me, it is sad that seldom anyone paints a picture of Jesus smiling. Didn't He did say something about bringing us abundant life and joy? People experience enough misery each week just by facing the basic challenges of everyday life. The church should be a people who bring hope and refreshment into peoples lives. The people of God should be the happiest people in the world.

It is such a joy to receive on a regular basis e-mails from people who introduce themselves as someone who "hasn't been to church in years," has "given up on God and the church," "loved God but hated church," "visited many churches but never felt wanted...but then we came to Midway." Others have mentioned a moral failure of some kind and had wondered if they could ever be forgiven and get their life on a positive track again. Then they were invited to Midway. Recently in our weekend worship gatherings we featured the real life-change stories of three individuals for just ninety seconds each. One had been delivered from drug and alcohol abuse, one had an abortion and had found forgiveness and love, and the other was a bishop over a

Mormon church just five years earlier but has found Christ and is now entering the gospel ministry.

It's these kinds of stories that we now live for. New life is what the gospel is all about. The gospel is the Good News that brings new life. We realize the gospel is not about robed choirs or ensembles, quartets or praise teams, pipe organs or contemporary bands, hymns from a book or choruses from a projector, bulky pulpits or thin-line stools, designer suits or faded jeans with flip flops, chandeliers or strobe lights, pews or theatre seats, cathedrals or converted warehouses. We believe these things are nothing but tools that build a bridge to a particular culture. They are not holy or unholy. They are not sacred or sinful. At Midway, we are committed to use the bridges that connect to the lives of the generations with the largest percentage of unbelievers in our community. The gospel of Jesus Christ is their only hope. I'm convinced that every church must know the demographics of its own community in order to be consistently effective for any length of time. In some parts of the world, this is not as much of an issue, but here in the cultural melting pot of America, it's a big issue.

Midway is itself quickly becoming a melting pot of cultures and races. That in itself is a problem in many churches since the church remains perhaps the most segregated institution in America. Much of the disagreement and struggle about worship styles is actually a fight against cultures rather than theology. For us, though, it is often the very reason many choose to call Midway home. They're glad to be a part of a church that values people without qualification. I must admit it is refreshing to pastor people of varied cultures and races, and I have seen our diversity bring out the best in so many.

Another major shift is the mass of young families that are migrating to Midway. Many went to church as children and are experiencing a renewal of faith in their family as young adults. There is a long line at the security check-in stations for the preschool and children areas. Teenagers are bringing their "weird" friends from school, many who have never been inside of a church building. They are occasionally adorned with metal studs and rings in strange places, and often have a skateboard for transportation. Instead of running them off, we purchased professional skateboard ramps for them to use. A few of the church members left the church, refusing to allow their kids to intermingle at church with such sinner! Some said, "We bring our kids to church to get them away from those kinds of kids!" However, we are seeing many of these young people come to Christ and grow in their faith. Our average age has now dropped from about fifty to thirty-seven.

Another major change at Midway is the clarity and common knowledge of our vision. Our Five Star Focus is both the purpose for our existence and the process by which we live our lives and gauge our effectiveness.

We exist to:

1. Love God
2. Love People

3. Serve the World

4. Invite Others

5. Give Generously

We have gone to great lengths to help Midway attendees understand why these five things are important and how each step effectively leads us toward a life on mission with Christ. It's a life that demonstrates excellence in the basic disciplines of the Christian life. They are stretched to do such things as personally invite every family within a one-mile radius of their home, experience twenty-one days of fasting and prayer, help start a new church, or join a short term mission team to minister somewhere around the world.

After just a few weeks of attendance, most people can quote our Five Star Focus and they know we are committed to do ministry with excellence. Before they decide to officially join us, they know we are committed to do more than sing songs and preach sermons. We are committed to worship our awesome God—both privately and corporately. We are committed to take the church to the people, both in our own community and around the world. We are on a journey, and that journey is more important than life itself. It's a journey that will take thousands to heaven until the return of our Lord. That journey requires the personal involvement and generous giving of every person who is a member. We are not interested in adding new names to our membership so we can boast about our membership size. We are not interested in religious parasites moving in; people who see membership as a title for the privileged few who enjoy the benefits of an organization without giving and serving. We want people to come who'll adapt to a life of becoming a missionary; people who'll live every day with a commitment to bring Jesus into every circumstance of life. We are consistently evaluating and adjusting to help people live that kind of life.

There is a final subject of improvement I want to mention. It's in the area of numerical growth. I want to note that in 1985, Midway reported only sixty-eight people in its small group ministry and was struggling to pay the bills of the church. We now regularly reach more than thirteen hundred in our small group ministry. Some 1,500-1,600 people now gather each weekend for worship.

Every step of advancement from 1985 until now can be directly linked to a risk the church was willing to take. There was a step of faith and a willingness to change. Midway has not grown by accident, but through intentional efforts to move to the next phase of our journey. Our attendance is at an all-time high. Our baptism rate is at an all-time high. The number of first-time visiting families is at an all-time high. The number of people involved in meaningful ministry is at an all-time high. Our vision and hope for the future is at an all-time high. In short, it's a NEW day at Midway! And that's a good sign that God is doing a NEW thing among us. Our story is just beginning and the best is yet to come!

Chapter 6, part 2 (Marty)

"that the sharing of your faith may become effective by the acknowledgment of every good thing which is in you in Christ Jesus.."

Philemon 6

"Do not seek to follow in the footsteps on the men of old; seek what they sought."[1]

Matsuo Basho

"The voice of the spiritual leader, when echoing the heart of God, resonates in the hearts of those who are already seeking after God."[2]

Erwin McManus

Moving Forward

As of this writing, we are just over two years after the implementation of the last transition. We no longer consider ourselves to be "in transition," but to that we have transitioned. I believe that we are on the track that God wants us on and that we are more prepared than ever to be driven by the wind of the Spirit of God.

Our body has developed a great understanding that we cannot just throw open the doors and say, "Ya'll come!" to the surrounding communities, therefore, we are looking for various kinds of opportunities to impact the lives of those

[1]- McManus, 224.
[2]- McManus, 194.

around us without waiting for them to show up at the door. Though we have no "visitation program," our "on mission" status is stronger than ever.

Community Involvement

During the last couple of years, we have made inroads into the subdivisions around us and into two of the local elementary schools. In one subdivision we painted mailboxes at a time when homeowners were about to be fined by the HOA for rusty posts. A group of fifteen or so spent the better part of a morning delivering homeowners from the wrath to come and established goodwill in the community-not to mention with the HOA.

During the Christmas season, we spent a Saturday in two different subdivisions wrapping gifts. At no charge, a person could bring their entire stash of gifts and have them very well wrapped, ready to be given to their friend, co-worker or loved one. This particular event did not draw a huge number of people, but it did allow for extended conversation on more than one occasion. After all, it takes a while to wrap twenty gifts.

Over the past year we have been given the opportunity to impact the lives of public school employees in our area by twice a year hosting lunches for them. In the fall and in the spring, when the weather is perfect in the Southeast, we cater a lunch for all employees from teachers to administrative to custodial. This has opened innumerable conversations with teachers and administration and not a few parents as well.

After a recent event, we received a note from one of the teachers indicating that the ministry has created a lot of discussion as to what each of their churches might do to better be salt and light in the community. That is exactly the kind of impact that we were hoping to have.

Having been informed of the cost that teachers must bear out of their own pockets for classroom decoration, we gave gifts one year to each teacher in a particular school...a hundred dollars per classroom. Needless to say, they were very grateful!

As of this writing, November 2007, we are beginning to see the first fruits of our efforts. People who had been detached from church or unchurched are attending and slowly coming to faith in Christ. Interestingly, they are coming from areas where we have not done specific ministry. It is as if we are sowing in one place and God is giving us a harvest in another! It seems that those with little to no church background take longer to come to Christ. Maybe it is a more skeptical outlook, a desire to thoroughly check out the claims of Christ or the authenticity of the people, but whatever the reason-very few people have come once and accepted Christ. I find that I must be patient as these were the very people we had in mind when we started the transition! Regardless, our goal remains to engage our culture in as many ways as we can.

For Christmas of 2007 we have been given the opportunity to take a drama/musical outdoors to a local resort where we can give a clear, culturally meaningful presentation of the meaning of Christmas. This resort, Lake Lanier Islands, hosts a drive-through light exhibit during the entire Christmas season and people come by the thousands to see the animated displays. For two consecutive weekends (Friday-Sunday) we will do four performances a night, twenty-four in all, in one of the more highly visible parts of the park-one of only two places where people can actually get out of their cars. Though we will not be giving an invitation, the gospel will be clearly presented in a compelling way that brings the need to make a decision into focus.

The success of this effort resulted in being asked to come back at Easter to do a morning service at the one thousand-seat amphitheater. Keeping in line with our goal of communicating the gospel in ways that unchurched and unsaved people can grasp, we will use drama in conjunction with music and speaking to present the story of Jesus and His resurrection.

The U.S. and Beyond

One area that has continued to be a vital component is our investment in national and international mission efforts. Our partnership in Sells, Arizona, on the Tohono O'odham Nation is expanding as are partnerships in an Eastern European country and the Russian republic of Tuva, the latter of which is a ground level entry into a mostly unreached people group. God has opened doors for us to be able to relate to the local government administration there while preparing to refurbish a city park and build a community center.

Despite our being many hours of difficult travel away from this region, we are convinced that God is leading us to partner there and are being obedient to Him.

Another unexpected event happened recently when our pastor of worship and administration announced, with his wife, that they would be going to spend a year with our missionary in Eastern Europe teaching and training new worship leaders and teaching English as a means to present the gospel to students and young professionals. He will take a total of eighteen months leave of absence-six months to raise support and then the full twelve to serve.

Each week I can sense the anticipation with which our folks come to the services. I hear over and over how welcomed newcomers feel when they attend and how quickly they feel as if New Bethany is home. People are eager to get into God's Word and to allow it to permeate their lives. The gospel is being shared through both lives and words and people are being saved. We see new faces each and every week and our guests are sticking with us.

Each week seems to present a new opportunity or some new door opening for God's work. New Bethany, through the power of the Holy Spirit, has proven willing to journey on faith into the unknown and I hope that never changes. It has been an amazing ride.

I would like to say that the transition has resulted in a doubled attendance and a couple of hundred baptisms. The reality is that our attendance now has crept back to almost pre-transition level, though we are trending up a little at a time. In this I must confess some disappointment that we have not had explosive growth, but that will be covered in my final chapter.

To Each His Own

If you are a pastor reading these words, it is my prayer that you would soberly consider any transition that you might undertake to lead your church. It is very painful, but worth it because of obedience. You must be willing to leave the results with God and be content in knowing you have done His will.

If you are a church member, I hope that you have received a more clear understanding of what many pastors go through in making decisions that affect a church. If your pastor is attempting to lead you church in a potentially difficult direction, then support him with all your might. Yes, you might lose a few friends, but you'll gain the approval of the One who distributes eternal rewards.

If you are a seminary student or young pastor, please understand that it takes time to earn trust. It takes time for your people to gain enough confidence in you to follow you through the valley of the shadow of death. If your motivation is to be a success story or have articles written about you in *Outreach* magazine, or be invited to the denominational speaking circuit, then please go into the secular business world. Shepherding involves loving your sheep and being willing to lay your life down for them, not using them to promote your own ego or fill some personal void or emotional need. The concept of using a church as a stepping-stone to bigger and better things is about as foreign to the word of God as marshmallows are from motor oil. To follow in the footsteps of Christ, hirelings need not apply.

Understanding the Times and Seasons

Chapter 7, Reflections from Todd

My journey at Midway has taught me much about the times and seasons through which God seems to operate. Many leaders fail to lead their organizations through major times of transition successfully because they don't understand what to do, why to do it and what it will take. They often don't understand how people "process" the information that ultimately leads to real change. They function as if they can plant a seed today, without first tilling the ground. Then tomorrow they expect to reap a great harvest without enough time for the seed to germinate. I have learned that most people have to hear something twenty to twenty-five times before they understand what someone is really saying. Many will finally seem to understand and be willing to embrace a particular change. Still, after the change is actually implemented they will say, "Oh! I didn't know that's what you meant!"

The fact is that the way people process a new concept or idea is very much like the process an acorn goes through to become a mighty oak. It often takes years, not months, to transition from the idea stage to the stage where there is real change, growth, and effectiveness. There will be seasons of drought, floods, fires, and storms that will leave their mark during the journey. In his book, *Transitioning*, Dan Southerland emphasizes the thought that any pastor expecting to transition a church from one philosophy and culture to another should commit at least four years to the transitioning phase. I agree! If a pastor will not make a long-term commitment to a particular local church, then a major transition should not be attempted. Too often, pastors are looking for a "quick fix" rather than a long-term solution, and they aren't willing to go through the necessary seasons in order to experience a great harvest. They would often rather have a "High Attendance Sunday"—which is almost always followed by a low attendance—than to make in-depth changes that might seem counterproductive in the short-term, but will bring effectiveness two or three years down the road.

When God created the heavens and the earth, He placed the sun, moon and stars in the heavens, not only to provide light, but to establish "signs and seasons, and for days and years" (Gen. 1:14). God has established all of life to operate on a seasonal and cyclical basis. The most obvious are the seasons of winter, spring, summer and fall. For a farmer to ignore the seasons and choose to plow in the rain, plant in the winter snow, and still expect to harvest in the early spring would show either his ignorance or arrogance. He either doesn't know anything about farming, or he chooses to ignore reality and act as if he is wiser than God.

Our own personal lives also go through numerous seasons from the time we are born until the time we die. No particular season is evil or good. They all simply work together to keep life moving forward. Understanding this principle is foundational to successfully lead any church or organization to be effective for any extended period of time. When the demographics and culture of a particular community begin to change, the church should be the first to identify those changes and develop an effective strategy to meet people where they are with the gospel. In 1 Chronicles 12:32, the Bible speaks of "...the sons of Issachar who had understanding of the times, to know what Israel ought to do." Little else is mentioned about these particular men, but they obviously made a great contribution to the foundation of the early establishment of the nation of Israel, because they understood the season in which they lived and knew what to do during that season. For some reason, however, many church leaders today have a tendency to stick their heads in the sand, and completely ignore the value of understanding the changing times. Others simply preach against the changing seasons, as if, by doing so, they can prevent them from coming.

Every leader should become an expert at understanding the historical cycles, patterns, seasons and personality of the church, organization or department he or she leads. It's also important to know the patterns of social culture of the people in the church and the community. When leading a church through transition and change, there are few factors more influential than understanding these issues. Being a student of these things will likely need to be a lifetime habit, since they are constantly changing. Not only must the leader understand these things, but they must be packaged and communicated to the people in the church regularly if the leader expects to maximize the number of people who remain on the journey. It's been said that people accept change or embrace change for one of only two reasons. They either learn enough that they want to change, or they hurt enough they have to change. Effectively helping the people understand the history and demographics of their own church and community will go a long way in helping them be open to change.

To go a step further, it's actually important to develop a culture of change as a part of the DNA of the church, because just as the demographics and culture is in constant change, the effective church will also be in constant change. The church must always understand what cultural season they are living in, if they expect to effectively communicate the gospel message to the masses. It may be a cliché, but, the mission of the church really is "to communicate a never-changing truth to an ever-changing world."

A Word to the Willing

Now I want to speak directly to those of you who see the need to lead your church to intentionally transition to a more culturally connected style and philosophy of ministry. There are several issues to consider.

What needs to be done?

1. *Every church must come face to face with their history of effectiveness or ineffectiveness.*

Many church leaders live in a world that doesn't exist. They often perceive themselves as being much more effective than they actually are. This "reality check" is often painful, but is very necessary if a church ever expects to become truly effective. A church should look at such numbers as their growth patterns, first-time visitors per week, new converts and new people getting involved in ministry.

2. *Every church must define effectiveness.*

A fellow pastor recently stated to me, "I have been able to stay at the same church now for over twenty-five years because I have never messed with the music! We still do the same stuff we've always done!" To him, effectiveness was the absence of conflict over music. By the way, the music isn't the only thing he hasn't changed in twenty-five years. Even though the community he serves in is one of the fastest growing communities in the Southeast, his church has been on a plateau for many years. However, he feels successful because he has been able to stay there for a long time. The people still love him, partly because he hasn't led them to change in order to be truly effective at reaching people far away from God. However, traditional churchgoers feel very much at home under his leadership.

3. *Every church must get out of the church building and take a ride or a walk down every street in the community.*

Pray for the people who live on every street. The church must get a fresh new vision for the people God has called them to reach. Too often, the only time believers think about their mission is when they are in the church building. A little research will show that in most areas in America, less than fifteen percent (sometimes much less) of the population is in a church on a given weekend. Seldom is the percentage more than twenty percent. For those who don't know Christ, the church is their only hope; however, the church must remember and reconnect with those in their mission field.

4. *Every church must plan and develop a strategy with the unchurched in mind.*

Every missionary in every country around the world must introduce the gospel within the culture where they live and serve. God has clearly established a moral law and the church must uphold that law. However, in most cases around the world, a people's culture is not a violation of God's law. God is not a "one culture" God who has only one race of people, one language, one style of clothing and one style of music that is acceptable. Jesus died for the sins of the whole world, and Jesus is the common factor that can bring people together. However, that doesn't necessarily mean they must change cultures in order to be right with God. The church too often views every culture but its own as ungodly. Perhaps a fresh look at John the Baptist is needed to remind us that while man looks at the outward appearance, God looks at the heart! We must not be afraid to meet people right where they are with the gospel.

Why Change Things?

1. *Because the unchurched deserve a church in their area that is committed to reaching them.*

Rare is the church that will baptize three thousand in one year, much less in one day, week or month. I realize there was a unique movement of God in the early days of the church as described in the book of Acts. Two thousand years later, though, thousands of churches in America baptize no new converts in an entire year, yet most of them will consider no change in the way they do things. In today's church, not only is there often the absence of the real moving of the Spirit of God, there is also a complete disconnect between the church and the sinners Jesus called the church to reach; much like the disconnect between the Pharisees and the teachings of Jesus in New Testament times. My question for a church unwilling to change is, "Does that church even care that the people in their community are going to hell?" Every man, woman, boy and girl deserves a church nearby that is committed to loving them and reach them with the gospel of Jesus Christ. Too many churchgoers are so self-righteous and judgmental, they find it difficult to rub shoulders with sinners the way Jesus did.

2. *Because the church often doesn't reflect the demographics of its local community.*

In many cases, churches in large American cities die and ultimately close their doors because—as a result of urban sprawl and racial exchange—all of "their kind" of people and prospects moved away. Sadly, most church leaders either lack the courage or desire to effectively lead their churches to embrace, love and reach *all* people in their communities. It is understandable that many people may prefer to connect to and worship with others who are most like them culturally; however, a church in a racially changing area shouldn't wait until it's almost empty before attempting to connect to the next wave of people moving in. Many churches exist in the midst of thousands of people within a few miles of their doorsteps, yet they feel like their days of growth are over. They will often receive offerings to reach people of other races in other nations, but refuse to reach people of other races down the street. That's hypocritical! Often, concerned churchgoers feel they have to ask permission from church leaders before they invite someone to church from a different race, or someone who's guilty of a particular sin. What a shame and disgrace! Every church's philosophy should be: "As long as a person is breathing, you can bring them, and we will love them. If they aren't breathing, it's too late for them! Take them to the morgue!"

3. *Because the sacrifice of Jesus demands more than dead religion, and believers need to be able to die and meet God knowing they have given their best to reach others with the gospel.*

The current church scene in America does not paint a pretty picture. In the name of "holiness" and "doctrinal purity" the traditional church has developed an isolationist mentality that ignores the unchurched, ignores reaching the younger generation, ignores the realities of culture, ignores their own ineffectiveness, and ignores groups in the body of Christ other than their own. Make no mistake, this generation of saints will be held accountable for reaching this generation of sinners. Selfless and courageous leadership can reverse the current trends. The church must—once again—develop a passion to reach unbelievers. A passion similar to that of John Knox, who prayed, "God give me Scotland, or I'll die!" Right doctrine and right living, connected to the heart of God, should lead to a relentless passion to love and reach people without Christ.

4. *Because the cultures of our society are changing so rapidly, the church cannot afford to go to sleep at the wheel.*

I have come to the conclusion that at some point, the church became more interested in having religious worship gatherings than in "effectively" reaching people with the gospel message. We continue to send missionaries around the world to reach people groups that have five percent or more who profess to know Christ. I think that is great, but I also think we must move forward with great urgency to reach this next generation who are now approximately age thirty or younger.

What Will It Take?

1. *It will take a moving of the Spirit of God.*

The church belongs to Jesus, and I am certain He wants every local assembly to be effective. Every pastor will need to hear from God about specific changes and directions for the church in which they are responsible. Transitioning into effectiveness is not about simply developing some new programs or changing music styles. It not about copying what some other church is doing. It's about seeing with the eyes of God, loving with the heart of God and serving with the power of God. In short, the church is to be a movement of God to build the kingdom of God. Many disagree about the workings of the Holy Spirit in today's church. Some groups seem to focus most of their attention on the Holy Spirit's signs and wonders, while others almost deny His very existence. However, one thing is for sure. The church has no power to be a part of God's redemption plan without the presence and power of the Holy Spirit (Acts 1:8).

2. *It will take a leader committed to take risks, lead change, love people and manage conflict.*

All four of these qualities will be required in great abundance from the leader who attempts to transition a church into effectiveness. All of these things will be required in spite of the personal pain and criticism that will certainly flow in the leader's direction. The changes must be led from a biblical basis and a passionate vision to reach people, yet, there'll still be some people that all of the explanation in the world will not convince. As a result of change, a church may double or even triple the amount of new people who come to Christ, but all some people will notice is that their favorite song isn't being sung as often as before.

3. *It will take resources.*

I am speaking about people, money and time. Sometimes people are a double-edged sword in our lives. My greatest joys and deepest sorrows in life have involved people. In jest, I once heard a pastor say, "Being involved in ministry would be wonderful if I didn't have to deal with people!" I must say that on certain days, I understand that statement. Sometimes people will be difficult, hurtful and even cruel. However, I want to take this opportunity to say that without a core of people who have believed in me and the vision God has given me, I couldn't have made the journey thus far. Some of them are paid staff, but they have gone the extra mile to serve with excellence. Some are my own family members, who have been constant cheerleaders. Others are people I had never met until a few years ago and now, because of our journey together, I cannot imagine living life without them. They have relentlessly walked through this journey with me. They have sacrificed many things to help me lead effectively. They have sacrificed time and money. However, in some cases, they have sacrificed so much more. Some have sacrificed other friendships with people who were vehemently opposed to this new vision that burned within me. Others have sacrificed the approval and respect of family who opposed our new direction. Still, others have overlooked their own agendas, opinions, preferences and cultures, and have added more value to our journey than I can describe.

Many people who are above the age of fifty have chosen to stay and invest in a church that is committed to reach the younger generation. For them, the music is too loud, too unfamiliar and it's no longer "church music," meaning Southern gospel or traditional in nature. They miss the organ and hymnals. They don't like the flashing lights. They would prefer to trade our theatre seats back for our pews and to them, some people's attire often seems a bit too irreverent. However, they have chosen to stay and invest the remainder of their lives to reach a people group they do not fully understand, but that they love nonetheless. They serve much like the missionaries who invest their lives to reach a people group somewhere around the world. In short, at some point throughout our journey, these people have truly become missional in their philosophy of life.

The people who have walked this journey with me have made what is often a difficult road not only bearable, but meaningful. I will be forever grateful for their loyalty, friendship and devotion. There is a generation of young people in West Georgia whose lives will be brighter and whose eternities will be heavenly as a result of their sacrifice. May people just like them rise like a mighty army from the pews of churches throughout our nation to win a battle that is definitely worth the fight.

On Faithfulness

Chapter 8, Admonition from Marty

"The fruit of Spirit is...faithfulness."

Galatians 5:22

"It is required of stewards that a man be found faithful."

1 Corinthians 4:2

"We shall reap if we do not lose heart."

Galatians 6:9

The purpose of this chapter is to encourage pastors. Like many, I have had the experience of attending a conference and coming back ready to change the world. Even taking into consideration the admonition to "take back the principles that will work in your setting" perhaps you still ran into Sister Bertha or Brother Fred who was just convinced that shifting the "Faithful Few" class down the hall one room was certain to herald the reign of Antichrist. The amount of time it takes for visionary balloons to deflate can be measured in nanoseconds.

There are far too many pastors who suffer from destroyed dreams and shattered goals resulting from efforts that go unrewarded in this life or, possibly, using the wrong method to evaluate their performance. The subject matter at hand needs to be subjected to scriptural scrutiny.

Evaluations

My formative pastoral years were with the period of the church growth movement from the late 1980s to the mid-1990s. My bookshelves still bear witness to my reading during that time. Along with most pastors I was just interested in "growing my church," or ministry area. I was really no better off philosophically than the people who measure church health only by the number of baptisms and whether the budget is being met. Neither of these units of measure, of course, is proposed in the New Testament.

In every opportunity for ministry I've had to think through how God actually quantifies success. Part and parcel with our transition mindset was a discussion as to what it would mean to be successful. Would it take an increase in attendance? More professions of salvation? More baptisms? Is it good preaching? Is it more people involved in Bible study? Exceeding the budget every year? Will God evaluate the church differently than He evaluates the pastor of the church?

Of course each of these can be a marker and for many they are well-tracked indices of productivity (though I remain concerned that our consumer-oriented society has invented a direct correlation between the size of a church and God's blessing). In evaluating my own ministry I found that measuring success by a non-biblical standard brought me much turmoil, but if I was using a biblical standard then I tended to be at peace and the only biblical standard of success that I've been able to find is faithfulness (faithful obedience).

In addition to measurements of success, I had to answer a question to which I already knew the answer, but that always seemed to affect the way evangelism was done: Who is responsible to save the lost? Is it my responsibility to save them? What about the deacon chairman? The evangelism pastor? It seemed clear to me that God is responsible for He alone can save. Our responsibility is to get the gospel to the lost—it's a primary part of our job description (Matt 28:18-20, Acts 1:8). What I wanted to know was this: Were we being the most effective at taking the gospel to the lost and was merely vocalizing the tenets of the gospel as effective toward life change as demonstrating the gospel in word and deed? I believe that both are needed.

It's for this reason that I quit worrying about the numbers game. I always wish we were reaching more-I always wish that I personally was reaching more-but I will no longer evaluate whether we are successful based purely on numbers, be they baptisms, buildings or budgets. For me, success is being obedient-personally and as a church-to God's leading. It makes no sense and it might even be sin for a pastor to appropriate the responsibility of God in ultimate results. We can control planting, de-thatching, weeding and watering, but God gives the increase.

By the standards of success that are commonly used to evaluate who should speak at our conferences, whose book should be picked up by the publishing house or what church is worth emulating, Jesus was an unmitigated failure. When He left Palestine (Acts 1) His three-and-a-half years of public ministry had left a scant one hundred twenty committed followers, one suicide, open ridicule, no government influence and the official status of being a "sect" of Judaism-hardly the makings of a "How To" volume at Barnes and Noble. Of course, the entry of the Holy Spirit into the ministry of His people brought an explosion of sustained growth that has rarely been exceeded to this day. Unfortunately, that explosion is too often the standard of measure by which pastors, denominational leaders and others evaluate the success of pastors and churches. At a conference I attended a few years ago a consultant referred to a church that, for a period of months, had a *net gain of 1,000 new attendees per month*. Woe to the pastors who would evaluate their personal ministry by that standard. The kind of thinking that invites such a comparison makes no sense at all to me.

My deep down hope was that God did not merely use baptisms, bodies, buildings and budgets as the criteria by which I would be evaluated at my judgment. Surely, I thought, He would give credit for effort. I've even thought at times that I should get the same reward as pastors of exploding churches since I must have tried at least as hard as they did. It is not my fault if I have less personal ability to use!

To the Word

A survey of the New Testament gives little hint to what kind of growth patterns existed outside the day of Pentecost. We are told in Acts 2:47 that the Lord added souls each day; Acts 6:7 says that the number of disciples multiplied greatly in Jerusalem. It is probable that there was a period of exponential growth as the word of Jesus' resurrection spread so quickly that it could not be stopped.

But, once the early church record is exited and we examine the Epistles there is a dearth of the same kind of information. How many showed up for worship at Corinth? What was the Bible study enrollment at Ephesus? What was the size of those churches on Crete that lacked bishops and awaited Titus' assigned ministry? We are not told; not even given an estimate. We are informed in several places that the church met in this or that house which seems to indicate a small gathering of believers.

This must beg the question: Does our fixation on numbers have its roots in the biblical record? The evidence says it does not. Thus we must examine faithfulness as the primary measure of success. This should not surprise us as God has called us to faithfulness and those who enter into the kingdom are commended as both "good and faithful" not "good and successful." The one on the throne of eternity is called "Faithful" as well as "the Lord who is faithful" (Revelation 19:11, 2 Thessalonians 3:3).

One thing that gets overlooked is that faithfulness is not simply the bearer of fruit-faithfulness *is* the fruit. Galatians 5 teaches us that faithfulness ("faith" in some translations) is itself a fruit of the Spirit, while Paul also encourages us to "not grow weary in doing good, because in due season we will reap if we do not lose heart" (Galatians 6:9), and Jesus Himself positively noted of the church at Ephesus, "you have persevered and have patience, and have labored for My name's sake and have not become weary" (Revelation 2:3). Each of those harvest metaphors implies faithful obedience to the task.

In these days of number crunching and performance based evaluations, faithfulness has fallen on some rather hard times, though it still has not fallen out of favor with God. As a matter of fact, a further review at the character of God as revealed in His word might yet reveal to us why faithfulness is so directly tied to the work of the Holy Spirit in our lives:

"Therefore know that the LORD your God, He is God, the faithful God who keeps covenant and mercy for a thousand generations with those who love Him and keep His commandments" (Deut. 7:9).

"Trust in the LORD, and do good; dwell in the land, and feed on His faithfulness" (Ps. 37:3).

"O LORD God of hosts, Who is mighty like You, O LORD? Your faithfulness also surrounds You" (Ps. 89:8).

"O LORD, You are my God. I will exalt You, I will praise Your name, For You have done wonderful things; Your counsels of old are faithfulness and truth" (Isa. 25:1).

"Your mercies are new every morning; Great is Your faithfulness" (Lam. 3:23).

"God is faithful, by whom you were called into the fellowship of His Son, Jesus Christ our Lord" (1 Cor. 1:9).

It seems to be unarguable that God's path for our lives includes certain valleys designed to develop faithfulness through which God puts His power and character on display. Preoccupation with non-biblical measures of success only serves to distract from the development of His character in us-a development which lies outside our ability to easily quantify. When we remain faithful to the calling God has placed on us, walking in obedience to His leading-no matter how frustrating or lonely the trial-we know the pleasure of God whether we reach numerical goals or not.

Please understand that in no way is this call to faithfulness intended to provide an excuse for not bettering our own leadership skills. Consistently poor leadership practices cannot be called "faithfulness," nor is, "I'm just being faithful to the call," an excuse for unwise pastoral decisions or a place of refuge from ill-conceived actions. When God calls us to faithfulness, He is calling us to shepherd His flock among us with the same faithfulness that He exhibits toward us.

Faith

Attempting to lead a church through a major transitional phase will cause headache, heartache and sometimes questions about the very call to ministry. And, truthfully, it may not give the result for which we were hoping, but the question remains: Are we willing to be faithful in obedience simply because God has called us to it? I trust that we will be.

In the great faith chapter of Hebrews 11, we have listed the great men and women whom God holds up as examples to us. Following the introductory list of Abel, Enoch, Noah, Abraham, Isaac, Jacob and Sarah is an interesting qualifier. The writer says, "These all died in faith, not having received the promises, but having seen them afar off were assured of them, embraced them and confessed that they were strangers and pilgrims on the earth" (v. 13). The little phrase "not having received the promises" is key. It means that they were faithful to God even though they did not personally receive what God had promised. Instead, they were (and are) counted faithful because they died still seeing the promises from a distance. It was not their earthly success that God saw, it was their willingness to remain faithful to Him even when they did not experience the fullness of what He promised. We who are pastors face the same situation. Do we have the willingness to be faithful in obedience if it means that we die having only seen the promise of God and not having experienced it ourselves?

We all enjoy the stories of Adonirum Judson in Burma and Hudson Taylor in China and others who labor for years and years until God finally moved and many came to faith in Christ. But what if there had been no move of God? What if they had toiled and died in absolute obscurity having never been known by following generations? Was their faithfulness to God as pleasing to Him as the eventual harvest that was given? I have to say yes, since this is the clear implication of the New Testament. If the blood of the martyrs is the seed of the church, then there are many pastors who are planting blood, sweat and tears into a fallow and barren soil wondering why God is not sending fruit to their field who will be rejoicing eternally over blessing they longed for, worked for and hoped for but only saw from a distance.

And despite the hardship, there will come a day when God will say to them, "Well done, good and faithful servant: You have been faithful over one city, I will give you authority over ten cities! Enter into the joy of your Lord!" And it will have been worth it all.

Selected Bibliography

Frost, Michael and Alan Hirsch, *The Shaping of Things to Come*, Hendrickson Publishers (Peabody, MA), 2003.

Hybels, Bill, *Courageous Leadership*, Zondervan (Grand Rapids, MI), 2002.

Kouzes, James M. and Barry Z. Posner, *Credibility*, Jossey-Bass (San Fransisco, CA), 2003.

Maxwell, John, *The 17 Indisputable Laws of Teamwork*, Thomas Nelson Publishers (Nashville, TN), 2001.

McManus, Erwin Raphael, *An Unstoppable Force*, Group Publishing (Loveland, CO), 2001.

McNeal, Reggie, *The Present Future-Six Tough Questions for the Church*, Jossey-Bass (San Francisco, CA), 2003.

Slaughter, Michael, *Unlearning Church*, Group Publishing (Loveland, CO), 2002.

Southland, Dan, *Transitioning*, Zondervan (Grand Rapids, MI), 1999.

Stetzer, Ed and David Putman, *Breaking the Missional Code*, Broadman and Holman (Nashville, TN), 2006.

Van Gelder, Craig, *The Essence Of The Church*, Baker Books (Grand Rapids, MI), 2000.

White, James E., *Rethinking The Church*, Baker Books (Grand Rapids, MI), 1997.

Wright, Tim, *The Prodigal Hugging Church*, Augsburg Fortress Press (Minneapolis, MN), 2001.

Other Recommended Reading

Banks, Robert, *Paul's Idea of Community*, Hendrickson Publishers, Inc. (Peabody, MA), 1994.

Boice, James M., *Foundations Of The Christian Faith*, Intervarsity Press (Downer's Grove, IL), 1986.

Clowney, Edmund, *The Church*, Intervarsity Press (Downer's Grove, IL), 1995.

Colson, Charles and Ellen Vaughn, *The Body*, Word Publishing (Dallas, TX), 1992.

Cordeiro, Wayne, *Doing Church As A Team*, Regal Books (Ventura, CA), 2001.

Edwards, Jonathan and Edward Hickman (Editor), *The Works of Jonathan Edwards, Volume 1*, The Banner of Truth Trust (Carlisle, PA), 1834, 1995.

Frazee, Randy, *The Connecting Church*, Zondervan (Grand Rapids, MI), 2001.

Giles, Kevin, *What On Earth Is The Church?*, Intervarsity Press (Downer's Grove, IL), 1995.

Hirsch, Alan, *The Forgotten Ways*, Brazos Press (Grand Rapids, MI), 2006.

Horton, Michael S., *Where In The World Is The Church?*, Moody Press (Chicago, IL), 1995.

Hull, Bill, *Can We Save The Evangelical Church?*, Fleming H. Revell (Grand Rapids, MI), 1993.

Lewis, Robert, *The Church Of Irresistible Influence*, Zondervan (Grand Rapids, MI), 2001.

Macchia, Stephen A., *Becoming A Healthy Church*, Baker Books (Grand Rapids, MI), 1999.

Malphurs, Aubrey, *Developing a Vision for Ministry in the 21st Century*, Baker Books (Grand Rapids, MI), 1999.

Piper, John, *Let The Nations Be Glad*, Baker Books (Grand Rapids, MI), 1993.

Pope, Randy, *The Prevailing Church*, Moody Press (Chicago, IL), 2002.

Rainer, Thomas S., and Eric Geiger, *Simple Church*, B & H Publishing Group, (Nashville, TN), 2006.

Southern, Richard and Robert Norton, *Cracking Your Congregation's Code*, Josey-Bass (San Francisco, CA), 2001.

Stanley, Andy and Ed Young, *Can We Do That?*, Howard Publishing, Co. (West Monroe, LA), 2002.

Wagner, E. Glenn and Steve Halliday, *The Church You've Always Wanted*, Zondervan (Grand Rapids, MI), 2002.

Willis, Avery, Jr., *The Biblical Basis For Missions*, Convention Press (Nashville, TN), 1979.

Winter, Ralph D. and Steven C. Hawthorne (Editors), *Perspectives On The World Christian Movement*, William Carey Library (Pasadena, CA), 1992.

About the Authors

Todd Wright has been the Lead Pastor of Midway, in Villa Rica, Georgia since 1996. He holds a Master of Arts in Biblical Studies degree from Luther Rice University. He has a passion for the world, having served internationally 22 times in 13 nations in Central and South America, Africa, Europe, and the Middle East. Todd is also a leadership conference speaker with the International Leadership Institute. He has been married to his wife Lisa since 1982. They have two teenage daughters, Hannah and Olivia. They enjoy living on a farm in West Georgia. Todd can be contacted though Midway's website at www.midwaychurch.com.

Marty Duren has been in pastoral ministry since 1989, most recently as Lead Pastor of New Bethany (newbethany.org) in Buford, Georgia. Largely self-taught, he hopes to complete his undergraduate degree in time to jointly celebrate his 30th high school reunion. His desire to see the glory of God displayed to the peoples of the world has taken him to every inhabited continent and compelled him to engage unreached people groups such as the Tuvan people of Siberia. He has been married to the longsuffering Sonya since 1984 and greatly enjoys his three children, Beth, Timothy and Abigail. He enjoys reading, laughing, hiking and blogging (iemissional.com). Marty can be contacted via email, martyduren@hotmail.com.